Five Modern Japanese Novelists

Five

Modern

Japanese

Novelists

Donald Keene

COLUMBIA UNIVERSITY PRESS ■ NEW YORK

Columbia University Press
Publishers Since 1893
New York   Chichester, West Sussex

Library of Congress Cataloging-in-Publication Data
Keene, Donald.
   Five modern Japanese novelists / Donald Keene.
      p. cm.
   Includes bibliographical references and index.
   ISBN 0-231-12610-7 (cloth : alk. paper)
      1. Japanese fiction—20th century—History and criticism.
   2. Authors, Japanese—20th century. I. Title.

   PL747.65 .K44 2002
   895.6'34409—dc21

                                                    2002073412

∞

Columbia University Press books are printed on permanent
      and durable acid-free paper.
Printed in the United States of America
Designed by Lisa Hamm
c 10 9 8 7 6 5 4 3 2 1

Contents

Preface

The five authors whom I discuss in the following pages were men I knew and often met. I hesitate to call all of them my friends, not because there were disagreements, but because (in the cases of Tanizaki and Kawabata) our ages were so far apart that our relationship might be better characterized not as "friendship" but as repeated acts of kindness shown by two great writers to a young admirer. Mishima and Abe were close friends, and we met many times over an extended period of time. Shiba and I became acquainted some years after I had met the others, and although we met comparatively seldom, I thought of him as a friend; he certainly was a benefactor.

I should say how lucky I was to have arrived in Japan for study in 1953. At that time, there were few foreign students of Japanese literature, and famous writers, perhaps curious to see what we were like, graciously invited us to their homes and gave us freely of their time. Today it is by no means so easy for foreign students, even those who possess an excellent knowledge of the Japanese language and are better acquainted with Japanese literature than I was in 1953, to meet writers whose works they are studying. It is no longer unusual for foreigners to speak Japanese fluently, and the writers, like everyone else in Japan, are so much busier than they were fifty years ago that they have trouble finding time to meet foreign students of Japanese literature.

Early in my stay in Kyoto, I was lucky in having met by accident Nagai

Michio, who would later have a distinguished career and serve as minister of education. Through him I met his friend from childhood days, Shimanaka Hōji, the president of the publishing firm Chūō Kōron Sha, who in turn introduced me to many writers. I could not have had a better entrée into the Japanese literary world.

I confess that I did not in every case take advantage of the opportunities I was given to know writers better. I remember, for example, the disappointment of my meeting with Masamune Hakuchō, an author and critic about whom I would later write. A photographer, noticing Hakuchō emerge from a restaurant at more or less at the same time as myself, stopped us both and asked to take our picture. He then asked us to chat for a few moments in order to make for a more natural photograph. I could not think of anything to say to Hakuchō. I vaguely remembered his name but had never read a word by him. Hakuchō obviously had not heard of me and had nothing to say. We stood side by side for some minutes in dead silence. Finally resigning himself to the situation, the photographer took our picture anyway, and the photograph, showing us standing stiffly apart and staring glumly at the camera, appeared in the *Tōkyō shimbun*. Some months later, when I was doing research on the poet Ishikawa Takuboku, I discovered that Hakuchō had known him well. I realized that if I had asked him, he could have told me much of interest, but I had missed my chance. I never saw him a second time.

This was not by any means my only missed opportunity, but there is no point in enumerating the many times that ignorance kept me from seizing once-in-a-lifetime chances to get to know writers whom twenty years later I would treat as major figures in my books.

Fortunately, however, I did not miss *every* opportunity that came my way. In particular, I was lucky to have known the five writers described in this book. But it never occurred to me (curses!) that I would forget our conversations, so I made no notes, kept no diary. I remember many things, but it is likely I have forgotten even more. If I had a better memory or the assistance of a diary, I might have been able to recall fresh, never-before-recounted anecdotes about Tanizaki, Kawabata, and Mishima rather than those that already have appeared in my *Dawn to the West*, a history of modern Japanese literature. I also have repeated descriptions of works by these three authors from my earlier work, but I hope that this book will be read by persons who might be daunted by the bulk of my history. Perhaps, because of the different context, the repetitions will seem not only forgivable but welcome.

Five Modern Japanese Novelists

Tanizaki Jun'ichirō

(1886–1965)

Before arriving in Japan in 1953 I knew the name of only one living Japanese novelist, Tanizaki Jun'ichirō. It was by no means unusual at that time for a non-Japanese to be unfamiliar with contemporary Japanese literature, but I should have been better informed. I had studied Japanese literature as a graduate student at Columbia and Harvard and had taught Japanese for five years at Cambridge. I had published three books, including an introduction to Japanese literature that contains a chapter, "Japanese Literature Under Western Influence," in which I discuss several works by Tanizaki but none by any other living writer.

The causes of my ignorance were varied. First, I tended to prefer the classics to modern works, regardless of the language in which they were written. Perhaps this was the result of the humanities class I took at Columbia as a freshman and my admiration for my teacher, Mark van Doren, who wrote persuasively of the great books as the foundation of a "liberal education." I was also under the influence of the atmosphere prevailing at Cambridge, where at that time literary scholarship was almost exclusively directed at a study of the past. Finally, virtually the only works of Japanese literature that were available in readable translations were the classics.

What, then, made me particularly aware of Tanizaki? I had read several stories, including the celebrated "Tattooer," in English or French translation, and while in Hawaii during the war, I had read in Japanese his novel *Naomi (Chijin no ai)*. But more important than either of these experiences was a gift I received in 1951 from the great translator Arthur Waley, whose work had been an inspiration ever since I began the study of Chinese and Japanese. I got to know Waley while I was living in England, and on some occasion he gave me the three volumes of *The Makioka Sisters* (*Sasame-yuki*) that Tanizaki had sent him. The volumes, printed on conspicuously better paper than other novels of that time, were inscribed by Tanizaki to Arthur Waley. I guessed that Tanizaki had sent Waley the books hoping that the celebrated translator of *The Tale of Genji* would translate his own novel, often compared with *Genji*. Waley had no intention of making a translation — it had been years since he had translated anything from Japanese — and gave the books to me after reading them. It was difficult to obtain books from Japan at the time because of British currency restrictions, and I was delighted with the gift.

I took the first volume with me when I set out with three friends on one of the unforgettable journeys of my life — in a Land Rover, a British jeep, by air from the south of England to the French coast, then down to southwest France, and from there across to Italy, Yugoslavia, Greece, and finally Turkey, where the first Congress of Orientalists was held since the war. I read *The Makioka Sisters* in the back of the jeep when I could as it traveled over dusty roads or through rivers that had lost their bridges during the war. The frequent bumps in the roads interfered with my reading, and I had trouble also with the Kansai dialect used by characters in the novel. I did not encounter any Japanese on the way who might have helped me, but I persisted, and when I returned to England I read the two other volumes. I became convinced that *The Makioka Sisters* was a masterpiece and so described it in my book *Japanese Literature*, published in the spring of 1953 in England.

Later in 1953 my dream of going to Japan was realized, thanks to the Ford Foundation. Most foreign students chose to study in Tokyo, but I chose Kyoto, partly because I had heard that Tanizaki lived there. After my arrival in Japan I wondered how I might go about calling on him when a perfect opportunity came my way. In Tokyo I visited Edward Seidensticker (whom I had known when we were both at the U.S. Navy's Japanese-language school), and he told me he had just finished his translation of Tanizaki's novel *Some Prefer Nettles* (*Tade kuu mushi*). Not trusting the Japanese postal system, he asked if I would personally deliver the manuscript to Tanizaki when I returned to Kyoto.

Of course, nothing could have given me greater pleasure. On the appointed day I took the manuscript to Tanizaki's house in Shimogamo, a splendid Japanese-style residence. It was late summer, and as I sat waiting for Tanizaki to appear, I admired the garden and listened to an intermittent sound of what I later learned was a *shishi-odoshi*, or deer-frightener; falling water poured into a cup that, when full, made a sound like wooden blocks struck together. This was said to frighten away deer and made a pleasantly cool sound in the Kyoto summer heat.

Tanizaki appeared soon afterward. He was dressed in a kimono, as he was on almost every occasion when I saw him. He asked me about my work, and we chatted for perhaps an hour in a friendly manner. I did not know at the time that he was famous for his dislike of visitors. I also did not know that by and large he was uninterested in men. Although he would speak with me or with other men in an agreeable manner, as if interested in the conversation, his face would light up whenever a woman appeared. He told me once that during his years in Kyoto since the war, he had not made a single male friend. Not surprisingly, his stories set in Kyoto are notable for their female characters, who seem to have been based on women he knew.

Even at our first meeting Tanizaki spoke freely about his writings. I asked him particularly about certain events in *The Makioka Sisters*, rather expecting him to say, as some novelists do, that they were entirely invented or were composites of many events; but he confirmed without hesitation that each was described more or less exactly as it had occurred. I found other evidence of the factual reality of *The Makioka Sisters* at his funeral when the prototypes of the four sisters of the novel, one after the other, offered incense at the altar. When I learned that Tanizaki had died, I sent Mrs. Tanizaki a telegram of condolence. In my haste and agitation I addressed it not to Matsuko, her name, but to Sachiko, the name she is given in *The Makioka Sisters*, a slip suggesting that I had come to identify her completely with the character in the novel. Yet Tanizaki often voiced contempt for writers of autobiographical fiction and was sure that the work of an author was to invent.

Tanizaki invited me to dinner several times. I remember that on one occasion a particularly magnificent *tai* (sea bream) was served. It had a bump on its nose which, I was told, signified that it had passed through the whirlpool at Naruto. Like many of the delicacies consumed in the Tanizaki household, this was a gift from an unknown admirer. Many people cooperated to provide Tanizaki, a great gourmet, with the best in Japan. He also did what was necessary to ensure a suitable supply of provisions. When he moved to Atami from Kyoto to escape the cold winters, he was dismayed to discover there was nothing edible in Atami. He arranged, therefore, that every day a seat would be reserved for Tanizaki's food on the express train Hato. Someone in Kyoto placed the food on the seat, and someone else would retrieve it in Atami.

Tanizaki was recognized as belonging to a special world. Fukuda Tsuneari described how on a crowded train during the immediate postwar period, Tanizaki, Mrs. Tanizaki, and her sister occupied three of four seats in a compartment. The fourth seat remained empty as long as they were there; no one could muster the courage to intrude. It was not that the standees recognized Tanizaki or that he did anything to keep them from sitting beside him; rather, the atmosphere of civility they engendered in an otherwise free-for-all world seemed to forbid intrusion.

I can imagine the scene. All three are dressed in kimonos, not ostentatious but of obviously good quality, contrasting with the discarded uniforms and synthetic-fiber kimonos worn by everyone else. They smile and chat in low voices. Occasionally Mrs. Tanizaki takes some tidbit from her handbag and offers it to the others. Without making the slightest attempt to create an impression, they seem like incarnations of good breeding, conspicuous amid the pushing and shoving around them. Their manner suggests that something precious has survived the terrible years of the war and the postwar privations.

Surely there was no Japanese who seemed less likely than the young Tanizaki to metamorphose in his old age into this incarnation of Japanese decorum. He was born in Tokyo in 1886. His father was a dismally unsuccessful businessman who failed in every enterprise he undertook. The father seldom appeared in Tanizaki's works, but his mother, known as a beauty in her girlhood days and even much later, not only figured prominently in many published reminiscences but served as an ideal of feminine beauty, and the theme of yearning for a mother appears in many pieces. Tanizaki displayed his brilliance early. He was always the brightest pupil in his class. At the age of eight he composed a poem in Chinese celebrating a victory in the Sino-Japanese War. A teacher, recognizing the boy's genius, took him under his wing and guided him through the classics of East and West, including Buddhist treatises, the poetry of Saigyō, and Carlyle's *On Heroes*. Tanizaki's closest friend at school recalled that even at the age of eleven or twelve, they had discussed Kant and Schopenhauer. When regular classes were over, Tanizaki attended special schools where he studied English and Chinese. His knowledge of both languages remained with him for the rest of his life.

We are told of a character in a novel written in 1914 (when Tanizaki was twenty-eight) that although he tried reading the works of William James, Rudolf Eucken, and Henri Bergson, he had never managed to finish a single book. This was not because he had problems with foreign ideas: "No matter how difficult to understand a book was reputed to be, he had never once felt a book was difficult. After reading two or three lines he could guess everything that followed, and he would at once reject the book with contempt."*

Tanizaki's education almost ended with elementary school. His father was anxious to have him start earning money as soon as possible, but Tan-

---

*Except where otherwise noted, all translations are mine and were published in my *Dawn to the West* (New York: Columbia University Press, 1998).

izaki's teacher persuaded the father to let the boy take the entrance examinations for the First Middle School. He passed with such distinction that his father reluctantly agreed to the boy's continuing his education. His earliest writings appeared in the literary magazine circulated among students at the middle school. An essay published in 1902 startled his classmates by the assurance and vocabulary with which he criticized "oriental" pessimism. His insistence on joy as essential to human life was the first expression of the hedonism for which he later became famous.

Tanizaki was able to study at middle school by working as a *shosei*, a kind of combination houseboy and tutor, in the family of a restaurant owner. His humiliation at being treated as a servant would be recalled in the autobiographical story "The Boy Prodigy" (Shindō, 1916) and also in a very late volume of essays published in 1961, evidence of how deeply his resentment lingered within him. He was unceremoniously expelled from the household when a love letter he had addressed to a maid was intercepted.

In 1905 Tanizaki was promoted to the First High School. He enrolled in the division of British law, presumably in the hopes of proving that he was serious about getting ahead, as was expected of Meiji-period youths. He continued, however, to be active in the school literary society, and a story he published in its magazine about his first love was later developed into a novel. Details of this escapade are obscure, but a letter written in English to his brother at the time survives. It opens: "My Dear Brother: An evil accident which happened to me and her, obliged me to go to Hakone as soon as possible."

Tanizaki entered Tokyo Imperial University in 1908. He enrolled in the Department of Japanese Literature, known as a haven for students who chose not to study, and rarely attended classes. He took to frequenting the licensed quarters and contracted a venereal disease. He seemed indifferent to the plight of his family, who were annoyed not only because he failed to contribute to their support but also because they still had to provide him with food and a bed. He had established himself as an egregiously unfilial son. But he discovered the one remedy for his disgrace: in 1909 he began to write professionally for publication. He established his reputation with the short story "The Tattooer" (Shisei), published in the following year.

Years later (in 1956) Tanizaki revealed that the original setting of "The Tattooer" was contemporary, but he had shifted the period back to the Tokugawa era because the story did not work as a modern piece. This remark suggests how he would use the Japanese past in his writings. He had no desire to make the figures of the past come alive by attributing to them contemporary attitudes in the manner that authors of popular historical fiction did, nor did he attempt to preserve absolute fidelity to the facts, nor was he dependent on the past for materials because he lacked resources of imagination. He set his works in the past because this gave him greater scope for his imagination. Actions that might seem exaggerated if attributed to contemporaries were believable of people who lived at times when life was more brightly colored than in the present.

"The Tattooer" is entirely fictitious, and whether or not the background is historically accurate is irrelevant. What remains in the reader's mind is the intensity and the decadent atmosphere. Seikichi, the tattooer, is attracted to a girl when he catches a glimpse of her naked foot. We are told: "To his sharp eyes a human foot was as expressive as a face. . . . This, indeed, was a foot to be nourished by men's blood, a foot to trample on their bodies."* Tanizaki's foot fetishism is often coupled with his ideal of the beautiful but cruel woman. In his last novel, *Diary of a Mad Old Man* (*Fūten rōjin nikki*, 1962), he describes his perfect woman: "Above all, it is essential for her to have white, slender legs and delicate feet. Assuming that these and all the other points of beauty are equal, I would be more susceptible to the woman with bad character."†

---

*Jun'ichirō Tanizaki, "The Tattooer," in *Seven Japanese Tales*, trans. Howard S. Hibbett (New York: Knopf, 1963), p. 163.
†Jun'ichirō Tanizaki, *Diary of a Mad Old Man*, trans. Howard S. Hibbett (New York: Knopf, 1965), p. 27.

The slavish worship of cruel women is a frequent theme in Tanizaki's writings. In the early story "Children" (Shōnen, 1911), a group of small boys and one girl play at games involving sadomasochism. "Cops and robbers" is given a distinctive twist by the savagery with which the "robber" is punished. The most memorable of the games is the last. Up until this point the girl has always had to play the part of a victim, but this time she makes the boys her slaves. They eagerly trim her toenails, clean the insides of her nose, and even drink her urine.

In his novel *Jōtarō* (1914) the central character seems to be an alter ego for Tanizaki himself, although the work is in no sense confessional. While Jōtarō was at the university, he had read Krafft-Ebbing and learned that many famous men had been masochists. He was particularly fascinated by accounts of European prostitutes who gratify men by whipping them, demanding that the men worship their boots and indulging in similar varieties of amorous play. Unfortunately, there was almost no chance of finding a Japanese woman who would behave so cruelly. Tanizaki sometimes regretted that he had been born in contemporary Japan; it might have been easier in the Tokugawa era to gratify his "slightly abnormal" tastes.

Tanizaki married in 1915, a year after completing *Jōtarō*. It did not take long for him to begin behaving atrociously toward his wife, apparently because of her overly close resemblance to the traditional Japanese ideals of a good wife. He wrote that he had married in order to deepen his art, but soon afterward he openly stated that his marriage had been a mistake. In 1919 and 1920 he published several works of fiction whose subject is a man's murder of his wife. On the other hand, he found himself increasingly attracted to his sister-in-law, Seiko, who had un-Japanese features, un-Japanese gaiety, and un-Japanese waywardness.

The attraction that the West exerted on him is most clearly revealed in the story "The German Spy" (Dokutan, 1915), which describes his first European acquaintance, a shiftless Austrian with whom he studied French conversation. Tanizaki recalls in the story that previously he had been totally uninterested in Western painting and music: "Even while our gentlemen of letters were making a fuss over Gauguin and trumpeting the cause of exoticism, I was of the opinion that any Japanese who was interested in exotic art would do better to direct his attention to China or India." He goes on:

Two or three years later, however, I reached the point where I could not but shake off such stupid ideas. I discovered that as a modern Japanese, there were fierce artistic desires burning within me that could not be satisfied when I was surrounded by Japanese. Unfortunately for me, I could no longer find anything in present-day Japan, the land of my birth, that answered my craving for beauty. There was neither the overripe civilization of the West nor the intense barbarity of the South Seas. I came to feel utter contempt for my surroundings. At the same time, I thought I would have to observe more deeply, more intimately, the West, whose art was so infinitely greater than our own. I would have to seek from the West objects to satisfy my craving for beauty, and I was suddenly overcome with passionate admiration for the West.

Western painting and music had hitherto left me cold, but now they made me tremble with excitement at every contact. For example, the paintings of the Impressionist school . . . overwhelmed me by their powerful, intense character, so unlike the manner of expression of Japanese paintings, which are distinguished only by manual dexterity and totally lack content or stimulation. I could hear Western music only on the rare occasions when it was performed by Japanese, or in excerpts on phonograph records, but how directly and how grandly it sang of the sorrows and joys of human life as compared with the faint and somnolent sounds of the samisen, or the curiously perverse, retrogressive, superficial *hauta*, *jōruri*, and the like. Japanese vocalists sing in voices trained to produce unnatural falsetto tones, but Western singers sing boldly and with impetuousness, like birds or wild beasts, sending forth their natural voices so ardently they risk bursting their throats.

Japanese instrumental music produces a delicate sound like the murmur of a little stream, but Western instrumental music is filled with the grandeur of surging waves and has the intense beauty of the boundless ocean.

Once I had become aware of these truths, I felt an uncontrollable desire to learn everything there was to be known about the countries of Europe that have given birth to these many astonishing works of art and about the various aspects of the daily lives of the superior race of men living there. Everything labeled as coming from the West seemed beautiful and aroused my envy. I could not help looking at the West in the same way that human beings look up to the gods. I felt sad that I had been born in a country where there seemed no possibility that first-rate art could be nurtured. I grieved in particular over my misfortune that having been condemned to the fate of being born in Japan, I had chosen to make my life as an artist rather than as a politician or military man. And I made up my mind that the only way to develop my art fully was to come into ever closer contact with the West, if only by an inch closer than before, or even by totally assimilating myself into the West. In order to satisfy this craving I would go abroad if possible—no, going abroad would not be enough. The best and only way was to move there permanently, resolved to become one with the people of that country and to have my bones buried in its soil.

There could hardly be a more uncompromising admiration for the West than Tanizaki's in "The German Spy." Of course, this was a work of fiction, and the sentiments do not necessarily reflect Tanizaki's beliefs, but the tone carries conviction, and similar sentiments are found in other works. In *Naomi* (*Chijin no ai*, 1925), for example, Jōji's infatuation with Naomi is stimulated by her un-Japanese behavior, her un-Japanese features, and even by her name, which, by coincidence, is also found in the West. Tanizaki's fascination with his sister-in-law was similar to Jōji's with Naomi.

In the early 1920s Tanizaki began to be interested in films as an artistic medium. His first scenario, *Amateur Club* (*Amachua kurabu*), was filmed in 1920. It was a comedy and the star was none other than Seiko, his sister-in-law, who appeared in the first scene in a bathing suit. He once remarked that her feet were the most beautiful objects in the entire world.

Tanizaki moved to Yokohama in 1921 and led a totally Western-style life. He wore flashy clothes, notably red neckties, and boasted that he never took off his shoes all day long. A European friend of Seiko's taught him to dance, and dancing soon became a mania with him. He even encouraged his shy wife to dance. He reveled in the exotic atmosphere of the Yokohama Bluff and wrote stories and plays based on his experiences there. Although the newspapers reported that Tanizaki was about to leave for Europe, he postponed the journey until the autumn of 1923. Then his whole life was changed by an event that occurred on September 1, 1923: the Great Earthquake.

Tanizaki was on a bus when the earthquake struck. The bus veered wildly on the road, but he was not in danger. His first reaction was worry about his family. "However," he related, "at almost the same time joy welled up inside me. I thought, 'How marvelous! Tokyo will become a decent place now!'" He was sure that in ten years Tokyo would revive, as San Francisco had done after its earthquake in 1906, but this time as a far more imposing city:

Orderly thoroughfares; shiny, newly paved streets; a flood of cars; apartment houses rising floor on floor, level on level, in geometric beauty; and, threading through the city elevated lines, subways, streetcars. And the excitement of a great city, a city with all the amusements of Paris or New York, a city where the night life never ends. Then, and then indeed, the citizens of Tokyo will come to adopt a purely European-American style of life, and the young people, men and women alike, will all wear Western clothes. This is the inevitable trend of the times, and whether one likes it or not, this will happen.

Tanizaki was pleased to think that his daughter, now seven, would no longer have to sit on the tatami or constrict her body with an *obi* or wear heavy wooden clogs. She would grow up healthy and play sports. He saw the emergence of a new species of Japanese woman: "The change will be so great it will be almost as if they belonged to a different race. Their figures, the colors of their skin and their eyes will all become like those of Western people, and the Japanese they speak will have the ring of a European language."

The essay containing these sentiments was written in 1934, eleven years after making these predictions. He now admitted that his predictions had not come true, blaming this on the fact that Tokyo had not been as extensively damaged by the earthquake as he had supposed. The old habits had also proved unexpectedly tenacious: even though Western food was now more generally available, people still preferred Japanese food, and nine out of ten women still wore kimonos. He no longer hoped that the future would bring a greater degree of Westernization. He confessed also, "Now that Tokyo has at last become Westernized, I have bit by bit come to dislike the West. Instead of pinning my hopes on the future, I think nostalgically of the Tokyo of my childhood."

The change in Tanizaki is generally ascribed to his move from Yokohama to the Kansai region. Although in 1923 he was at the height of his infatuation with the West, he had begun to be intrigued by the old Japan, much as a foreigner is captivated by a Hiroshige print, and he thought he would enjoy visiting picturesque sites in the Kansai while waiting for Yokohama to be rebuilt. He gravitated naturally to Kobe, where the largest colony of Westerners in the Kansai region lived. But when the other refugees began returning to Tokyo and Yokohama, he stayed on. In 1926 he decided to settle permanently in the Kansai and declared he no longer felt any attachment for Tokyo.

He explained the change in terms of his preference for Kansai food, for the voices of Osaka women, for the prevailing atmosphere. Increasingly, too, he took pleasure in discovering in Kyoto or Osaka many of the customs that had disappeared from Tokyo but still lingered in his memory. The change in Tanizaki was qualitatively not very different from what many other Japanese men have experienced in their forties, when they discover the comfort of sitting on the tatami drinking saké with friends, or the taste of quite ordinary Japanese food, or the beauty of a Japanese lyric. In Tanizaki's case the process was more complicated because it was conscious, and the results were more important because they involved not merely his private life but also his work. Tanizaki's lasting reputation as a writer was established on the basis of what he wrote after moving to the Kansai; if all his earlier works were lost, his reputation would not be much affected.

It would be hard to exaggerate the importance of Tanizaki's accidental removal to the Kansai, although the change in his work did not occur right away. *Naomi*, his first novel after the move and the best book he had written in a decade, has many ties to his Yokohama period. It is a summing up of the craving for modernity, free love, and liberation from cramping old traditions that marked his earlier works but implicitly condemns Jōji for the unreasoning love for a coarse waitress that destroys a decent man. (This is reminiscent of Somerset Maugham's *Of Human Bondage*, published in 1915.) However, to its first readers, the book did not seem like a condemnation of the way of life it describes. Indeed, the term "Naomiism" was invented to evoke her appeal. The novel *Naomi* is not wholly successful, but it compels attention, and Tanizaki's characterization of Jōji as a "fool," in the original Japanese title of the work, *Chijin no ai*, indicated that he was emerging from his mindless worship of the West. When he visited Shanghai in 1926, he complained that the city had become infected with foreign ways.

Tanizaki, however, had no intention of abandoning the West completely. Examining the contention of certain orientals, notably Tagore, that the West was materialistic and the East spiritual, he concluded that "with the exception of the historical fact that Shakyamuni, Christ, and Mahomet, the founders of the three great religions, were all born in Asia, I am convinced that there is no basis for the claim that the East is more spiritual than the West."

Tanizaki believed that as the result of the introduction of Western literature, the special qualities of Japanese prose, especially its unspoken over-tones, would steadily disappear. He expressed no regrets over what he con-sidered to be an inevitable change. In the past, it is true, Japanese had come to appreciate Eastern traditions as they grew older, but by the time the present generation had reached full maturity, Eastern traditions might have disappeared, leaving them nothing to which they could return.

In 1929 Tanizaki completed *Some Prefer Nettles* (*Tade kuu mushi*). Some critics consider this to be Tanizaki's finest work, not only because of its intrinsic literary excellence, but because it presents subtly and effectively the great transformation in Tanizaki's life from a worshiper of the West to a believer in the value of the Japanese heritage. In this novel a man—rather like Tanizaki—discovers that he has returned imperceptibly into the world that he remembers from childhood.

The novel opens as Kaname stretches out on a reclining chair to read an unabridged English translation of *Arabian Nights*. Kaname, an alter ego of Tanizaki, is having an affair with a Eurasian prostitute. He does not object when his wife in turn announces that she is going to meet her lover, but even though their marriage is breaking up, some ties still join them—their son and Kaname's father-in-law. Kaname, more and more attracted to the old man, who enjoys performances of the puppet theater and lives in a typical Kyoto house, is intrigued also by Ohisa, the inarticulate mistress of his father-in-law. Ohisa's old-fashioned ways contrast with those of Kaname's wife, an "enlightened" woman under the influence of the West, and Kaname's interest in Ohisa parallels the rediscovery of the past. At the end of the book, as he lies inside a mosquito netting of the kind depicted in old prints, Kaname sees Ohisa enter the dimly lit room with an armful of Japanese-style books. He has come to share his father-in-law's tastes, anticipating Tanizaki's own "return" to Japan. Various events were modeled on incidents in Tanizaki's life at a time when he was moving toward a divorce, but the work was more prophecy than autobiography.

In the early 1930s Tanizaki wrote a series of stories that established him as the most accomplished writer in Japan, even though virtually no critic of the time recognized this. *Arrowroot* (*Yoshino kuzu*, 1931) reveals that he had found a subject and a language for expressing his changed way of looking at the Japanese past. The work contains several layers of time: the earliest goes back to the twelfth-century story of Shizuka, the mistress of the hero Yoshitsune, and her magical drum. This in turn is linked to the nō play *The Two Shizukas* (*Futari Shizuka*) of the fifteenth century and to the eighteenth-century drama *The Thousand Trees of Yoshino* (*Yoshino senbonzakura*). These different echoes of the past, unified by an undercurrent of belief in fox magic, give depth to the story and make it live in the reader's memory.

The transformation of Tanizaki from a popular author, known especially for his "diabolism," into the most important spokesman for the value of traditional Japanese culture was prefigured by the "return to Japan" indicated in *Some Prefer Nettles* by Kaname's awakened interest in his father-in-law's way of life.

Tanizaki remarried in 1931. He and his bride went to Mount Kōya, the center of Shingon Buddhism, for their honeymoon and remained there for four months while he studied Buddhism and wrote *A Blind Man's Tale* (*Mōmoku monogatari*), another important work set in the past. It would not have been surprising if happiness with his bride had been reflected in the work, but it was Mrs. Nezu, the neglected wife of a well-to-do Kobe cotton merchant, who inspired the work. In his introduction to the work Tanizaki wrote, "The lettering on the box, the cover, the title page, and inside title pages are from the brush of Mrs. Nezu." He had been informed also that the artist who drew the portrait of Chacha, the heroine of this sixteenth-century tale, based her features on those of Mrs. Nezu.

In the summer of 1932 Tanizaki confessed that he loved and even worshiped Mrs. Nezu. He declared in a letter,

To tell the truth, when I wrote *A Blind Man's Tale* and other stories last year, I had you in mind all the time, and I wrote as if I were the blind masseur myself. I feel sure that my art will continue to be enriched, with your help, and even if we are apart, my creative powers will spring afresh within me, in infinite abundance, as long as I can think of you. Please do not misunderstand me. It is not that you exist for the sake of my art but that my art exists for you. Please believe me when I say that if, by some good fortune, my art endures, it will be because it informs future generations about you.

Before long, he and his second wife were divorced, and he married Matsuko, the former Mrs. Nezu.

"The Reed Cutter" (Ashikari, 1932) tells of the author's visit to Minase, the site of the palace of the thirteenth-century emperor Gotoba. In a manner reminiscent of Mérimée describing Roman ruins in Spain as the prelude to his tale of Carmen, Tanizaki passes from the present-day loneliness of Minase to the Minase of fifty years earlier. A man emerges from the reeds of the river at Minase and relates the story of the beautiful but cruel Oyū-san. The old-fashioned nature of the narrative is accentuated in the original edition by ruled lines between the columns of text, by the occasional use of obsolete forms of the script, and even by the paper, all contributing to create the appearance of a book of the Meiji era.

The title of the play is not explained, but it is the name of a celebrated nō drama, and the structure of "The Reed Cutter" is strikingly similar to that of the *mugen*, or "dream fantasy," nō. But whatever influences the nō exerted, they are of relatively minor importance in a work that bears strong resemblances to others Tanizaki wrote at this time, in both the manner of narration—a monologue consisting of extremely long sentences—and the themes, some of which go back to Tanizaki's earliest writings. The narrator worships Oyū-san, the beautiful, often cruel, woman he serves as a slave; this is an almost overly familiar theme in Tanizaki, and it is a mark of his narrative skill that he convinces us Oyū-san is worthy of such extravagant attention.

The one story of the period that rivals "The Reed Cutter" in its brilliance is "A Portrait of Shunkin" (Shunkin shō, 1933). It was acclaimed as a classic when it was published, and this reputation has not wavered. Shunkin is a beautiful woman who teaches pupils to play the samisen. She takes sadistic pleasure in tormenting her senior disciple, Sasuke, who is absolutely devoted to her, despite this treatment. Shunkin is blind, but for Sasuke this only enhances her beauty. The climax of the story occurs when an unknown assailant disfigures Shunkin by pouring boiling water over her face. Acutely aware of the loss of her beauty, Shunkin refuses to allow anyone to look on her ravaged features. Sasuke always averts his glance, but he fears that one day he may accidentally see her face. To spare Shunkin this torture, he deliberately blinds himself by thrusting needles into his eyes. When he tells Shunkin that he also is blind, she reveals her affection for the first time, and he is blissfully happy.

"A Portrait of Shunkin" is more dramatic than "The Reed Cutter," and the characters are more convincing, but there is still much stylization. Tanizaki's intent was quite the opposite of the usual kind of historical fiction. He wrote,

> My wish has been to avoid imparting any modern interpretation to the psychology of Japanese women of the feudal period but, instead, to describe them in such a way as to recreate what those long-ago women actually felt, in a manner that appeals to the emotions and understanding of modern readers.

By maintaining this distance between the readers and the people of the work, Tanizaki kept intact the reserve and indirection that he felt to be an essential part of life in the Kansai region.

Tanizaki's most eloquent defense of the traditional aesthetics was presented in the essay "In Praise of Shadows" (In'ei raisan, 1933–1934). As the title indicates, he associated shadows (as opposed to the glare of electric illumination) with the old Japan, which he evoked with a nostalgia inconceivable in the Tanizaki of ten years earlier.

In 1935 Tanizaki began, with many misgivings, a modern-language translation of *The Tale of Genji*. He was torn between his desire to re-create the work for modern readers incapable of understanding the original and his fear that he was unequal to the task. The translation appeared in twenty-six fascicles between 1939 and 1941. While working on the translation, Tanizaki wrote little else.

The translation of an eleventh-century novel seemed to be quite uncontroversial, but Tanizaki was working during the national emergency of the war with China, and censorship was severe. The translation could not be published in its entirety because the chapters describing Genji's relations with Fujitsubo, the consort of the old emperor, were considered to be disrespectful to the imperial household. It is paradoxical that the supreme glory of Japanese literature was expurgated by men who professed undeviating allegiance to Japanese ideals.

In 1942 Tanizaki began to write his longest and probably best novel, *The Makioka Sisters* (*Sasameyuki*). The first episodes appeared in the monthly magazine *Chūō kōron* in January and March 1943, but in place of the next episode there was an editorial statement to the effect that further publication would not be in the national interest during the wartime emergency. Tanizaki continued to work on the novel, taking refuge from the wartime hysteria in the remote countryside. During the war years *The Makioka Sisters* was virtually all that he wrote. It is true that in 1942 he gave a radio talk celebrating the fall of Singapore, but his involvement in the war effort was minimal. He was able to survive without cooperating with the military because of his steady income from royalties. His hatred of the military went back to childhood days, and each new disaster of the war increased his bitterness.

Only after the war had ended could Tanizaki publish *The Makioka Sisters*. This should not suggest that the work expresses opposition to the ideology of the militarists; it is completely unconcerned with any ideology. Rather, *The Makioka Sisters* was banned because it described with nostalgia the Japan of the past when people were preoccupied not with the sacred mission of Japan but with marriage arrangements, visits to sites famous for cherry blossoms, and the cultural differences between Tokyo and Osaka. The leisurely pace exasperated those who insisted on a positive, exhortatory literature suitable to the heroic temper of the times, but the relaxed atmosphere was precisely what appealed to readers bored or exhausted by daily appeals to patriotism.

The Makioka Sisters was completed in 1948. It was awarded both the Mainichi and Asahi cultural prizes, and Tanizaki was invited to dine with the emperor. In November he received the Medal of Culture (Bunka kun-shō). The diabolist of a quarter-century earlier who wished to have his bones interred in foreign soil had been awarded every honor the Japanese establishment could bestow.

The narrative method of *The Makioka Sisters* is somewhat old-fashioned, but Tanizaki created a solid sense of reality that would be difficult to achieve with more adventurous techniques. He seemed intent on preserving for posterity the memory of Japan in the old days—not the Heian past or even the Japan of Tanizaki's youth, but the mid-1930s, when it was still possible for some Japanese to lead civilized, even cosmopolitan, lives. Like a chronicler anxious to record every detail of a way of life that is threatened with destruction, Tanizaki names the establishments where his characters shop and the numbers of the buses they take. The world of the Kansai ten years earlier is by no means idealized, but to Japanese living in the drab surroundings of the war years, a visit to see the fireflies in the mountains must have seemed a pleasure belonging to another life.

Many events in *The Makioka Sisters* can be verified by reference to Tanizaki's biography, but the interest is definitely not the product of a narcissistic absorption with the central character, in the manner of an I novel. The figure most closely resembling Tanizaki is neither a portrait of the author nor even a pivotal character. The comparisons made between *The Makioka Sisters* and *The Tale of Genji* are intriguing, but it is hard to imagine Lady Murasaki's novel without a Genji.

Tanizaki's next major work, *The Mother of Captain Shigemoto* (*Shōshō Shigemoto no haha*, 1949–1950), represented a return to the narrative style he had used in his antiquarian reconstructions of the past. The narration is often interrupted by the author's reflections on the texts of Tendai Buddhism, as explained to him by a learned monk, or by speculations on the materials available to modern researchers in their study of the Heian court.

It is almost as if Tanizaki was testing the limits to which he could push unnovelistic techniques in writing his work without losing the readers' interest. Yet such is the magic of Tanizaki's skill that even such interruptions contribute to the success of the novel.

After completing *The Mother of Captain Shigemoto*, Tanizaki began a second translation of *The Tale of Genji*, simplifying the style and including everything that had been deleted by command of the censors. The final volume of the translation appeared in December 1954. It is hard for us not to regret the four years he spent on the task, imagining the original works he might otherwise have written, but Tanizaki felt compelled to pay this second tribute to the masterpiece of Japanese literature.

It seemed to many readers that Tanizaki had concluded his career with this translation, but in January 1956 he electrified the public with the first installment of the novel *The Key (Kagi)* in *Chūō kōron*. That issue sold out immediately, and it was soon the chief subject of discussion in literary circles. The attraction of the novel lay in its outspoken descriptions of the sexual activities of a fifty-five-year-old professor and his forty-seven-year-old wife. The single-mindedness of the professor, who is determined to have his fill of sex before impotence overtakes him and directs his libido toward his own wife, leads to disastrous consequences for his health, but he persists.

Tanizaki's method of narration in *The Key* consists of two diaries, one kept by the husband and the other by his wife. The device is brilliantly handled and is given an ironic twist by each one's knowledge that the other is reading his or her diary. The work was praised in both Japan and Europe and America as unprecedented in its subject, but the absence of the themes found in Tanizaki's other works—longing for the mother, worship of the cruel woman, and so on—suggests that it was not very deeply rooted.

It seemed once again as if Tanizaki had ended his distinguished career, this time with a remarkable best-seller, but he surprised his audience. In 1961 and 1962 he serialized *Diary of a Mad Old Man (Fūten rōjin nikki)*. Although this novel did not create the sensation of *The Key*, it was artistically superior. This time, the theme was not love in middle age but love in old age. *Diary of a Mad Old Man* is a wonderfully comic work. Like many other great artists, Tanizaki ended his career with comedy. It is as if Tanizaki, still absorbed by the themes of his writings, now sees them at such a distance that they seem humorous. It is a captivating book, marred only by the weak ending: the logical ending, the death of the old man, was the one subject that Tanizaki could not treat with humor at this stage of his life.

Perhaps what distinguished Tanizaki's works most conspicuously from those of other major Japanese novelists of the twentieth century was his absorption with writing itself. His novels are not confessional, nor do they advocate any philosophy, either ethical or political, but they are superbly crafted by a master of style. No one would turn to Tanizaki for wisdom as to how a man should lead his life or for a penetrating analysis of the evils of modern society, but a reader seeking the special pleasure of literature and an echo in even Tanizaki's most bizarre works of eternal human concerns could hardly find a superior writer.

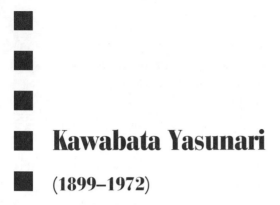

Kawabata Yasunari

(1899–1972)

I first met Kawabata Yasunari in 1953. He was only fifty-four, but he struck me as being very old and delicate, and photographs taken of him at the time, confirming this impression, suggest in their expression a deer frightened by a sudden flash of light. Yet I knew that he had another side. Far from being a recluse shut off from the harsh realities of the world, he had served since 1948 as the president of the Japanese PEN Club, a position that entailed not only skill and patience in maintaining peace at a time when political differences among the members divided the organization, but enduring hours of boredom at board meetings. He took this work seriously and regularly attended PEN Club meetings both in Japan and abroad, even though he did not understand any foreign language and simultaneous interpretation was not often available. Earlier in his career he had been active in publishing, and shortly before his death he campaigned vigorously for a candidate for the governor of the Tokyo Metropolitan District, riding from place to place aboard a sound truck. His last public activity was planning an international conference of scholars of Japan. This other side of Kawabata tends to be forgotten, especially by those who knew him and were accustomed to his long silences.

Kawabata's reputation in Japan, which went back to the 1920s and 1930s, was by 1968, the year in which he won the Nobel Prize in Literature, fully established; but many Japanese expressed surprise that a writer who seemed to them to be so specially and even peculiarly Japanese could be understood and appreciated abroad. The first translation of Kawabata's works into a European language seems to have been Oscar Benl's German version of "The Izu Dancer" (Izu no odoriko), published in 1942. But Kawabata's international reputation owes most to the fine translations by Edward Seidensticker, beginning with his version of the same story, published in 1955. Seidensticker's translations of *Snow Country* (*Yukiguni*, 1956) and *Thousand Cranes* (*Sembazuru*, 1959) established Kawabata's reputation abroad. Sales, however, were disappointing, and when Seidensticker submitted a sample translation of *The Sound of the Mountain* (*Yama no oto*), he was informed by his editor that the publisher had decided it wanted no more of Kawabata's "effete" writings.

The publisher's attitude changed dramatically, however, with the announcement in October 1968 that Kawabata had won the Nobel Prize in Literature. This was the first time since 1913, when Rabindranath Tagore was awarded the prize, that a writer from Asia had been honored. Probably the Swedish Academy did not know it, but 1968 had special significance to the Japanese. Just a hundred years earlier, in 1868, the Meiji Restoration had fundamentally changed both the culture of Japan and its position in the world. The award symbolically called attention to the emergence of Japanese literature as an equal among the literatures of the world, even though less than a hundred years earlier it had been completely unknown outside Japan.

In 1964, four years before Kawabata was honored, the Agence–France Presse announced that Tanizaki Jun'ichirō had won the Nobel Prize in Literature. Reporters flocked to Tanizaki's house in Yugawara to ask his impressions, but (alas) it was a mistake, and by the time Japan's turn at last came up in this geographically controlled competition, Tanizaki was dead. It is sad that this great novelist never received the prize, but Kawabata also deserved it richly.

It may have been an accident that Kawabata, rather than Mishima Yukio, received the prize. Shortly before his death in 1961, UN Secretary-General Dag Hammarskjöld read the translation of Mishima's novel *The Temple of the Golden Pavilion* (*Kinkakuji*, translated by Ivan Morris in

1958) and expressed great admiration in a letter to a member of the Nobel Prize committee. A recommendation from this source was not taken lightly. Again, in 1967, after I had unsuccessfully attempted to win the Formentor Prize for Mishima at an international gathering of publishers held in Tunis, a Swedish participant, a senior officer of the important publishing firm of Bonnier's, consoling me, said that Mishima would soon receive a much more important prize. That could only have been the Nobel Prize.

What prevented Mishima from obtaining the prize? In May 1970 I had dinner with friends in Copenhagen. Among the guests was a Danish novelist whom I had met at the time of the 1957 Tokyo PEN Congress. On the basis of the two or three weeks he spent in Japan on that occasion, he had acquired the reputation in Scandinavia of an authority on Japan. He was in a jovial mood that evening and confided to us proudly that it was because of him that Kawabata had won the Nobel Prize. He said that in his capacity as an expert in such matters, he had been asked by members of the Nobel Prize committee to give them the benefit of his opinions on contemporary Japanese literature; the committee seems to have decided that a Japanese would receive the award in 1968. Although the novelist had read very little Japanese literature, this did not inhibit his judgments. As I was vaguely aware from our previous meeting, he was extremely conservative in his political outlook, and this colored his opinions on other subjects. The recent turbulence in Japanese universities, widely reported in the foreign press, had made him extremely suspicious of all young Japanese, and when asked about Mishima, he reasoned that Mishima, being young, must be a leftist. He therefore spoke out strongly against Mishima, recommending instead Kawabata, whose age seemed to guarantee that he would not harbor radical political views. "And so," he concluded, "I won the prize for Kawabata."

I have no way of telling whether or not he in fact influenced the committee of the Swedish Academy, but a few clues suggest that his account may have been correct. Under the influence of the late Dag Hammarskjöld, the academy had been leaning strongly in favor of Mishima, as my informant in Tunis had indicated, but then, seemingly at the last moment, it changed its mind. Although (in accordance with regulations) three works by Kawabata were listed in support of his candidacy for the prize, comments were made on only two of them; nothing more than the name of the third, the novel *The Old Capital* (*Koto*), was given, suggesting that up until this moment, the committee members had favored Mishima and had therefore not bothered to read a third work by Kawabata, even though *The Old Capital* had been translated into German and Danish.

I confess that at the time I was greatly disappointed that Mishima did not win the prize. In retrospect, one might even say that he killed himself because he had failed to receive the recognition he desired above anything else in the world. But one could also say that Kawabata killed himself because he did win the prize, a burden he found too heavy to bear. Even though I grieve over the deaths of these two great authors, I now believe that the Nobel committee, for whatever reasons, chose wisely, that Kawabata, more than Mishima and more even than Tanizaki, deserved to be the first Japanese to win the Nobel Prize in Literature.

When Ōe Kenzaburō in 1994 became the second Japanese recipient of the Nobel Prize in Literature, he contrasted the literary tradition to which he belonged with that of Tanizaki, Kawabata, and Mishima—authors who, he stated, had chosen to write "pure literature," as opposed to the engaged writing practiced not only by himself but also by Ibuse Masuji (who wrote a novel about the atomic bomb dropped on Hiroshima), Ōoka Shōhei (who described in detail his experiences during the Pacific War), and Abe Kōbō (who wrote about such subjects as the alienation of the individual from society).

Ōe was not alone in this conviction. On several occasions when I have given a lecture in Japan on a subject such as the appreciation of Japanese literature in foreign countries, during the question period after the lecture somebody has asked me why foreigners translate only works that are redolent of *kachō-fūgetsu* (flowers, butterflies, the wind, and the moon), a term for the conventionally admired sights of nature found in traditional Japanese works of literature. It is obviously not true that only works characterized by flowers and butterflies have been translated, but I know what my interlocutor means. For so long, the appreciation of Japanese art in the West has been expressed in terms of the damnable adjective *exquisite*, which, in praising a work, reduces it to minuscule dimensions. Yes, the haiku is very short and by no means as powerful as an epic poem; yes, the most flawlessly executed netsuke does not compare with a masterpiece by Cellini, let alone an example of heroic sculpture; but a haiku that is no more than exquisite, a netsuke that, although charming, suggests nothing of larger dimension, is no more than a toy.

For Japanese authors whose writings are intended to be political gestures, even the deliberate ugliness of a novel like Kawabata's *The Lake* (*Mizuumi*) does not absolve it from the charge of being permeated with flowers and butterflies. These authors do not want to be praised for their flawless use of suggestion or their poetic evocations of nature; they refuse to embellish their works with such typically Japanese features lest they not be taken seriously. One can sympathize with their determination to transcend the particularity of being Japanese, but surely only the least sensitive reader would ever suppose that the novels of Tanizaki, Kawabata, and Mishima were nothing more than exquisite.

Kawabata suffers most from the demand that the writer be engagé. In an autobiographical account of 1934 he wrote,

> For me love, more than anything else, is my lifeline. But I have the feeling that I have never taken a woman's hand in mine with romantic intentions. Some women may accuse me of lying, but it is my impression that this is not a mere figure of speech. And it is not only women I have never taken by the hand. I wonder if it isn't true of life itself as far as I am concerned?

When preparing to write the novel *The Asakusa Crimson Gang* (*Asakusa kurenai dan*), a work about a cheap and rather sordid entertainment quarter of Tokyo, Kawabata walked the streets of the tawdry neighborhood, notebook in hand, at all hours of the day and night, but as he later wrote,

Although I spent the night in the park a number of times, all I did was walk. I never became acquainted with any of the young delinquents. I never addressed a word to the vagrants, either. I never set foot inside any of the cheap restaurants. I visited every one of the thirty-odd amusement houses, but took my notes from a seat in the audience and did not talk to the entertainers. . . . I never stood at the entrances to the flophouses around the park and never went into the cafés.

Kawabata's detachment, suggested by this passage, was such that after the Great Earthquake of 1923 he calmly wandered through the streets of Tokyo for weeks, inspecting the burned-out ruins and making mental notes of sights from which most people averted their eyes. But he was far from impassive. He wrote,

I desire to go not to Europe or America but to the ruined countries of the Orient. I am in large measure the citizen of a ruined country. No sight of human beings has stirred my heart as much as the endless queues of earthquake victims, looking exactly like refugees. . . . Perhaps it is because I was an orphan with nowhere I could call home that I have never lost my taste for melancholic wanderings. I am always dreaming, though I never manage to forget myself in any dream. I am awake even as I dream, but I hide this with my taste for back streets.

In November 1949, in his capacity as president of the Japanese PEN Club, Kawabata visited Hiroshima to inspect the damage caused by the atomic bomb. He seemed impassive before the terrible sights, and this impression of serene tranquillity with respect to everything except his own internal anguish was confirmed in the eyes of unfriendly observers when Kawabata spent time sightseeing in Kyoto on his return from Hiroshima. Kawabata later explained,

I wondered if I was not guilty of a contradiction in having gone to see the sights and art of the old capital on my way back from the horrible ruins left by the atomic bomb in Hiroshima. . . . But I cannot think there was any contradiction. I am, after all, the same person. Perhaps Hiroshima and Kyoto are the two poles of Japan today. I have been examining two such disparate sights at the same time and would like to examine them even more carefully. It goes without saying that looking at old objects of art is not a hobby or a diversion. It is a matter of life and death.

Kawabata said several times that he wanted to write a novel about the atomic bombs dropped on Hiroshima and Nagasaki. He said that regardless of whether or not he ever wrote such a novel, the fact that he had come to want to write it gave him a feeling of being alive. He never wrote about the bombs, but the collection of art that he started to form after the war grew until it became a major holding. He once described how a small object of art—a hand sculpted by Rodin, a nō mask, or a tea bowl—could sustain him when he spent the night at his desk. For this deeply sensitive, deeply feeling, but sometimes inarticulate man, art was not only a consolation but another voice.

During the course of his career, Kawabata wrote in different styles on different themes, but unlike Tanizaki, Mishima, and even Abe, he wrote no works of historical fiction, surprising for a man so committed to the Japanese tradition. Again, unlike Tanizaki and Mishima, he had served for a time as the spokesman for an avant-garde movement, and he did not abandon its techniques even at the end of his career. The seeming contradictions between Kawabata the eulogist of "beauty and sadness" (to use the title of one of his late works) and Kawabata the scenarist of the first avant-garde Japanese film or between Kawabata the preserver of Japanese tradition and Kawabata the explorer of ruined streets give his writings a complexity that made him a fit representative of modern Japanese literature and a worthy recipient of the Nobel Prize.

Few modern Japanese writers have grown up under unhappier circumstances than Kawabata did. By the age of three, he had lost both his parents. Four years later his grandmother died, and two years after that his sister died, leaving him alone with his grandfather. Attending funerals became so routine a feature of his life that Mishima (at whose funeral Kawabata presided) called him *sōshiki no meijin*, the master of funerals. This name also was the title of one of his earliest published works (1923).

The boy grew up at Minō, north of Osaka. I remember that Kawabata's face lighted up with pleasure when I mentioned once that I had visited the waterfall in Minō Park; he said he used to pass it every day on the way to and from school. There cannot have been much pleasure on returning from school to the house he shared with his grandfather. Kawabata's first work, "Diary of a Sixteen-Year-Old" (Jūroku sai no nikki), describes twelve days in May 1914, a week before the grandfather died. According to the afterword Kawabata wrote in 1925 when he first published the work, he had found the completely forgotten manuscript in an uncle's storehouse. He wrote, "I confronted the honest emotions of a forgotten past. But the grandfather I had described was uglier than the grandfather of my memory. For ten years my mind had been constantly cleansing my grandfather's image."

After a stylistic examination of the diary, some scholars opined that despite Kawabata's insistence on its authenticity, it was probably composed in 1925. Perhaps the most convincing evidence to support their conclusion is that the style of the diary, unlike that of other examples of Kawabata's juvenilia, is free from the stylistic flourishes one would expect from a bookish boy of fifteen. But regardless of the date of composition, it is an extraordinary evocation of the relations between a boy and his dying grandfather. The love—and the disgust—that the helpless invalid arouses in the boy is conveyed by the choice of details.

Perhaps the best-known passage is one in which the boy returns home and finds that his grandfather, now blind and almost unable to move, has been waiting impatiently for him to return. The grandfather asks the boy to bring the urine glass and put his penis into it:

I had no choice but to expose him and do what he asked, though it went against the grain.

"Is it in? Is it all right? I'm starting now. All right?" Couldn't he feel his own body?

"Ahh, ahh, it hurts. Ohh. It hurts something terrible." It hurt him to urinate. His breathing was so labored it sounded as if it might stop any minute, but there rose from the depths of the urine glass the sound of the pure water of a valley stream.

"Ohh. It hurts." The pain seemed more than he could bear. As I listened to his voice I felt the tears come to my eyes.

The water had boiled, so I gave him some tea. Coarse tea. I had to prop him up for each sip he drank. The bony face, the white hair ravaged by baldness. The quivering hands of bones and skin. The Adam's apple of his scrawny neck, bobbing up and down with each gulp. Three cups of tea.

It is hard to believe that a boy who was much under the influence of old-fashioned literature could write so simply about the death of his closest relative. But some details, such as the hope he expressed that if he kept writing the diary until it reached a hundred pages his grandfather would recover, ring true.

Kawabata's first published story, "A View of the Yasukuni Festival" (Shō-konsai ikkei, 1921), was in a totally dissimilar mood. It is the story of a circus equestrienne and her friends, told in a Modernist manner. The conversations are fragmentary and sometimes cryptic; Kawabata deliberately made it difficult to read. As a story it is immature, but the jagged style in the manner of Paul Morand's Ouvert la nuit (1922) attracted attention, and the author's noninvolvement with the characters—typical not only of this Modernist style but also of Kawabata's oeuvre—was praised as well.

Kawabata's most important work of this period was the story "The Izu Dancer" (Izu no odoriko, 1926), the work that not only brought him fame but remains the one for which he is most remembered even today, more than his novels. In order to shake off the depression of being jilted by a girl he had intended to marry, Kawabata went on a walking tour of the Izu Peninsula in the autumn of 1918. He fell in with a group of traveling entertainers and was touched by the readiness with which they accepted him. He was especially gratified to overhear several of the performers agree when discussing him that he was "nice"; he had convinced himself that no one had ever really liked him. It is hard to believe from the beauty of the face in photographs of Kawabata as an old man that when young he was almost grotesquely ugly. Being painfully aware of his ugliness, he also was relieved to discover that it did not bother the troupe.

The narrator of "The Izu Dancer" is attracted to the girl who plays the drum. He thinks of asking her to spend the night in his room, but when by accident he sees her emerge naked from the steam of an outdoor hot spring, he realizes that she is still a child, despite her grownup clothes and way of arranging her hair. This discovery, far from disappointing him, frees him of constraint, and he happily accompanies the troupe to Shimoda, at the end of the Izu Peninsula, where they part. Aboard the ship that takes him back to Tokyo, he weeps, but not out of sadness.

The popularity of "The Izu Dancer" has been attributed to its being a rare example in modern Japanese literature of the pure love of adolescents. Although the student hopes to sleep with the dancer, he is relieved, even purified, when he realizes that she is too young for lovemaking. She represents the romance of travel, rather than romance itself, and it is better that the ideal not be tarnished. Kawabata was attracted throughout his life to virginal, inviolable women. These were by no means the only women he described, but they seem to have represented for Kawabata the essence of beauty.

Kawabata dismissed his Izu stories (including "The Izu Dancer") as being no more than "traveler's impressions." This statement, made in 1934, reflected the extreme diffidence he always showed with respect to his works, but perhaps it was also his conviction. At the time he wrote "The Izu Dancer," he was deeply involved with the New Sensationalists, a Modernist school. He insisted in articles he wrote for the movement that "newness" was all and expressed boredom with established patterns of expression:

Our eyes burn with desire to know the unknown. Our mutual greetings are expressions of delight in being able to discuss whatever is new. If one man says, "Good morning," and another responds, "Good morning," it is boring. We are weary of literature unchanging as the sun that comes up from the east today exactly as it did yesterday. It is more interesting for one man to say, "The baby monkey walks along suspended from its mother's belly," and the other replies, "White herons really have long talons, don't they?"

Kawabata's most experimental work in the vein of the New Sensationalists was "Crystal Fantasies" (Suishō gensō), published in 1931 but never completed. In this work Kawabata practiced the stream-of-consciousness techniques that the Japanese Modernists associated with Joyce. Years later he revealed that he not only had read the Japanese translation of *Ulysses* but also had bought a copy of the English text and compared the two. The influence of Joyce, though not lasting, was considerable. In "Crystal Fantasies" Kawabata indicates with parentheses the unspoken reflections of the characters, and the long paragraphs apparently reflect influence from Proust, directly or through his friend the novelist Yokomitsu Riichi. Although this work is unlike anything Kawabata wrote later in his career, the imagery and even the language are curiously consistent. Here is the beginning of one of the parenthetical streams of thought:

The boy who made the doctor smile was really nice. The consultation room of her father, a gynecologist. The white enamel of the operating table. A great big frog with its belly turned up. The door of the consultation room. The white enamel of the doorknob. In the room with a door with a white enamel knob there is a secret. I feel it even now. The enamel washbasin. About to touch her hand to the white enamel doorknob, she inadvertently hesitates. The room has doors, any number of them, going every which way. White curtains. One morning, while on the excursion of our girls' school, I saw a classmate washing her face from a white enamel basin, and suddenly I felt I wanted to love her like a man.

The inspiration for these seemingly random associations is given a few lines later when the name Sigmund Freud is mentioned. The woman whose stream of consciousness is being reported has not had a child—to the disappointment of herself and her husband—and her reflections on reproduction later on are occasioned by the fact that her male dog is serving the female dog owned by another woman. The title of the story, "Crystal Fantasies," is a reference to a crystal ball that a fortune-teller uses to see the past and the future. Kawabata's failure to complete this work was typical of him. Many of his stories were never completed; others had chapters added or subtracted before Kawabata decided they had reached their final form.

Perhaps the form he found it easiest to employ was the short-short story. Between 1921 and 1972 Kawabata wrote 146, calling them *tanagokoro no shōsetsu* (stories that fit into the palm of one's hand). Every form is represented, ranging from the O. Henry story with a trick ending to the most fragmentary evocations. The best succeed in creating an unforgettable atmosphere in a few sentences, like crystallizations of the themes in his novels. Kawabata's last work, written just before he committed suicide, was the reduction to the length of a "palm of the hand" of his novel *Snow Country (Yukiguni)*.

Kawabata, who for years had led an extremely private life, began in 1933 to take a more active part in the literary world. To his surprise, he was appointed in 1934 to the Literary Discussion Group (Bungei kondan kai), organized by a former head of the Public Security Division of the Home Ministry. Kawabata's appointment to the group signified that the authorities considered him "safe." The ultimate purpose of the group was to control literary production by instituting cooperation between the government and certain writers, but on the surface it appeared to represent a serious attempt to promote a "renaissance" of Japanese literature.

In 1937 Kawabata's novel *Snow Country* received a prize from the Literary Discussion Group. By this time, the repressive nature of the government's intentions with respect to literature should have been clear, but Kawabata did not decline the prize. At the very least, he may not have been aware that he was being used; but at the same time, he continued to publish articles insisting on the importance of freedom of speech and even of a spirit of rebelliousness. Kawabata wrote, "Without a rebellion against conventional morality there can be no 'pure literature.'" His detachment was a fundamental part of himself, but when he spoke on issues affecting writers, he was liberal.

Kawabata's writings during the 1930s were in no sense nationalistic, nor were they aimed at ingratiating himself with the military. On occasion, the censors deleted words or phrases in his works, but on the whole he was able to write as he pleased without worrying about their reactions. In the late 1920s and early 1930s, when proletarian critics dominated literary criticism, Kawabata never openly denied the value of leftist writings, though he was clearly unsympathetic to their manner. Less than ten years later he was associating with the right-wing leaders of the "literary renaissance," but he himself had changed very little, and when the Literary Discussion Group decided not to award its prize to Shimaki Kensaku because he had earlier opposed "national polity," Kawabata protested, saying it was quite beyond the capacity of the awards committee to ascertain whether any pro-Marxist tendencies still lurked in the depths of Shimaki's heart.

At irregular intervals between 1932 and 1934, Kawabata published "Letters to My Parents" (Fubo e no tegami), addressed to the parents he had never known. He tells why he had been unwilling to have children, for fear they might inherit the "orphan's disposition" from which he suffered. He declared that he was more comfortable with animals than with people. Toward the end of the last letter, he returned to a childhood memory. While his grandfather lay dying, the boy had escaped from the gloomy house night after night. The thought of his cruelty in leaving the old man alone had continued to torment him over the years. The letters conclude with the description of the death of a friend, a painter. Kawabata, with a practiced hand, closed the friend's eyelids.

His next work, published the month after the five letters to his dead parents, was "Lyric Poem" (Jojōka, 1932), a work devoted to musings on death that is almost Surrealist in its construction. Writing in 1934, Kawabata said that "Lyric Poem" was his favorite among his recent works. It is at once a distillation of his thought up to this time and an insight into his future work. He reveals his growing absorption with Buddhism, especially as a poetic and artistic system:

> Compared with the vision of the Buddhas and their lives in the world beyond as depicted in the Buddhist scriptures, how very realistic is the Westerner's view of the other world! And how puny and vulgar. . . . It has seemed to me of late that the visionary passages in the Buddhist scriptures that describe past and future worlds are incomparably beautiful lyric poems.*

He wrote in an autobiographical account published in the same year:

> I believe that the classics of the East, especially the Buddhist scriptures, are the supreme works of literature of the world. I revere the sutras not for their religious teachings but as literary visions. . . . I have received the baptism of modern Western literature and I have imitated it, but basically I am an oriental, and for fifteen years I have never lost sight of my heritage.

Despite this avowal, undoubtedly sincere, Kawabata was far from attempting a return to the Japanese past. "Lyric Poem" draws on Christianity as well as Buddhism. The literary techniques are also those of modern European literature as practiced by Joyce and other contemporaries Kawabata had read, and even the details (as in the psychic vision a woman has of her lover) are drawn from a nonoriental world:

---

*Yasunari Kawabata, "Jojōka, Lyric Poem," trans. Francis Mathy, *Monumenta Nipponica* 26, nos. 3–4 (1971): 292.

You were listening to the music of Chopin. The walls of your room were pure white. Hung on opposite walls were an oil painting by Koga Harue and a print of a snow scene by Hiroshige. The wall tapestry, an Indian cotton print, had a pattern of birds of paradise. The covers on the chairs were white, but a greenish leather could be seen underneath. On both sides of the gas stove, which also was white, there were what looked like drawings of kangaroos. An album of photographs on the table was open to a picture of Isadora Duncan performing a classic Greek dance. On the whatnot in a corner of the room were some carnations left over from Christmas.

Despite the exotic touches—Chopin, birds of paradise, kangaroos—Kawabata found something Japanese, even specifically Buddhist, in the scene. The insistence on whiteness had a special meaning: far from thinking of white as the absence of color, he believed that it contained all the colors. Again, the childlike simplicity of Koga's Surrealist paintings struck him as being rooted in what he called "the old-fashioned oriental weakness for the poetic. A mist of distant yearning flows over the surface of the mirror of the intellect." He concluded, "They are not merely children's stories but vivid dreams of the surprise evoked in a child's heart. They are extremely Buddhistic."

Kawabata moved back and forth between the worlds of East and West. He never manifested the unconditional admiration of the West found in Tanizaki's early works, but he never rejected the West, either. Like the painter Koga Harue—who at the outset of his career used a palette similar to that of Paul Klee, moved to "oriental" colors, then returned once again to occidental colors, only to show renewed interest in oriental traditions shortly before his death—Kawabata's development was by no means a linear "return to the East" after an initial fascination with occidental Modernism.

In the spring of 1934 Kawabata visited the Yukawa Hot Springs. He paid a second visit in the autumn of the same year, and it was at this time that he began writing his most famous novel, *Snow Country*. The first chapter of the novel appeared in a magazine published in November 1935, and he published subsequent chapters in a variety of magazines until May 1937, apparently considering that each chapter could be read independently of the rest. The work was acclaimed by the critics and sold well. Kawabata had hitherto been known mainly for his critical essays, but this novel established him as a major novelist. Although everyone assumed that the book was complete, he added chapters in 1939 and 1940 and one last chapter in 1947.

The plot of *Snow Country*, like that of other successful works by Kawabata, is at once simple and elusive. A well-to-do dilettante named Shimamura returns late one autumn to the hot spring in the mountains he had visited six months earlier. After the train has passed through a long tunnel into the "snow country," it stops at a station where a girl in the same compartment asks the station master to look after her younger brother. When Shimamura arrives at the hot spring, a geisha, Komako, comes to his room at the inn. She has missed him more than he has missed her. She spends more and more time in his room, sometimes sober, sometimes very drunk. Although Shimamura is strongly attracted, he seems incapable of loving her. He also is attracted to Yōko, the girl he saw on the train. At the end of the novel there is a fire, and Yōko, who is in the burning building, leaps from the second story. Komako gathers her in her arms. Shimamura stands by helplessly, a bystander as always.

Komako, a woman of strong emotions and open sensuality, dominates the work. She is Kawabata's most successfully drawn female character, and if he had written no other work, this portrait would have earned him the reputation of being a master of feminine psychology. Yōko, although she appears only briefly, is almost equally appealing, but Shimamura is a cipher: the main thing we learn about him is that he poses as an expert on European ballet, even though he has never attended a performance. This special interest coincided with Kawabata's fascination in the 1930s with the dance. The dates of Shimamura's visit to the hot spring also coincide with Kawabata's, but he denied the importance of whatever models may have existed for the story:

The events and the emotions recorded in *Snow Country* are products more of my imagination than of reality. Especially with respect to the emotions attributed to Komako, what I have described is none other than my own sadness. I imagine that this is what has appealed to readers.

Kawabata once said that *Snow Country* could have been broken off at any point. He had originally intended to write no more than a short story, but some material was left over, and he incorporated it in the story he wrote for a different magazine. One chapter led to the next. Even after he wrote the concluding chapter in 1947, he thought he should have written more about the relations between Komako and Yōko. Readers may have trouble understanding precisely what happens at the end of *Snow Country*, but the effect is appropriate to a notably elusive work.

The glory of this novel is the evocativeness of its style. Almost everything that a more realistic author would have included in his account of the relations between Shimamura and Komako is either omitted or stated with such economy that the text must be read carefully. Kawabata relied on the possibilities for ambiguous yet expressive communication innate in the Japanese language. The conversations are not sparkling or even erotic but tend to be almost perversely indirect. Even as Komako insists that she is about to leave Shimamura's room, we can sense her intention not to budge from his side. *Snow Country* conveys—perhaps better than any other modern Japanese novel—the special charm of the Japanese woman, and not only of the geisha. It would be hard to name a work of classical literature to which Kawabata was indebted, but the prevailing impression is close to the Heian writings. It is Modernist in the free associations that skip from one perception to the next, but the ending is as tantalizingly obscure and aesthetically satisfying as any creation of traditional Japanese art.

In 1938 a series of matches took place between the master of *go* and a young challenger. Kawabata, whose fondness for *go* went back to his middle-school years, reported the matches in newspaper articles published between June and December. He decided to rewrite the materials in the form of the novel *The Master of* Go (*Meijin*). This quite short novel, though begun in 1942, was not completed until 1954. Kawabata was attracted to *go* because a match is a thing of beauty even if it serves no useful purpose. The victor is by no means a young upstart eager to dethrone the old master, but despite his respect, even his reverence, for the old man, the defeat is foreordained. On one level *The Master of* Go is an effective, even exciting, account of men and their devotion to a game; on another level it is a statement by Kawabata on the nature of men's consecration to art. The old master and the new master immerse themselves completely in a game that has no political, economic, or social significance; this also was Kawabata's stance.

During the war years Kawabata attempted to understand the special character of the country for which so many men were dying. He saw similarities between the Muromachi period, an age of warfare, and his own. In 1948, reflecting on the war, Kawabata wrote:

> I am one of the Japanese who was affected least and suffered least because of the war. There has been no conspicuous change in my prewar, wartime, and postwar works and no noticeable break. I did not experience any great inconvenience because of the war in either my artistic or my private life. And it goes without saying that I was never caught up in a surge of what is called divine possession to become a fanatical believer in or blind worshiper of Japan. I have always grieved for the Japanese with my own grief: that is all. As the result of the defeat, that grief has permeated my flesh and bones. But the defeat actually brought freedom of the spirit and the sense of what it means to live in peace.
>
> I consider that my life after the war consists of "remaining years" and that these remaining years are not mine but a manifestation of the tradition of beauty in Japan. I feel there is nothing unnatural about this.

When during the war it became evident that Japan would be defeated, Kawabata's chief consolation came from the classics, especially *The Tale of Genji*. He recalled his service as an air-raid warden in these terms:

When I went out on patrol during an alert on nights when autumn or winter moonlight flooded little valleys where not a speck of human-generated light showed, *The Tale of Genji*, which I was then reading, drifted through my mind, and recollections of the people of long ago who had read *The Tale of Genji* in adversity shot through me. I thought I must go on living, along with these traditions that flowed within me.

Here is another recollection:

I would stand stock-still on the road in the cold of the night and feel my own sadness melt into the sadness of Japan. I felt there was a beauty that would perish if I died. My life did not belong to me alone. I thought I would live for the sake of the traditional beauty of Japan. . . . Such were my thoughts and I went on living. Perhaps the piteousness of a defeated country has provided me with an unexpected refuge by reinforcing the meaning of my life. . . . Perhaps I had to see the mountains and rivers of my country after it had been defeated before everything else could disappear.

Kawabata's postwar activity was, however, by no means that of a recluse. On the surface he was busier than ever, not only as a writer, but also as president of the PEN Club and even as the publisher of the Kamakura Library. His novels *Thousand Cranes* (*Sembazuru*) and *The Sound of the Mountains* (*Yama no oto*), published together in one volume, won the literary prize of the Japan Academy. Both are important, deeply moving works. He also published what have been termed "middlebrow fiction," serialized in newspapers, and two remarkable novellas, *House of the Sleeping Beauties* (*Nemureru bijo*, 1960–1961) and *One Arm* (*Kataude*, 1963–1964). The former is the story of a man named Eguchi who visits a secret house of assignation where old men, presumed to be incapable of sexual intercourse, lie beside heavily drugged, naked girls. The story of Eguchi's five nights spent beside these mute women is carefully structured, and nowhere else is Kawabata's genius for evoking beauty more conspicuously displayed. The naked women cannot be distinguished one from another by dress, jewelry, speech, or the other externals that normally enable us to form opinions about a person's background and character, yet each remains distinct in the reader's memory.

One Arm opens with these startling lines: "'I can let you have one of my arms for the night,' said the girl. She took off her right arm at the shoulder and, with her left hand, laid it on my knee."*

The narrator—one of Kawabata's rare uses of the first-person narration—converses with the arm even as memories of other women he has known come back to him. He and the girl's arm lie peacefully together for a time, but suddenly the narrator decides to attach the girl's arm to his own body: "In a trance, I removed my right arm and substituted the girl's." He sleeps, but when he awakes, he is terrified to see his own arm lying on the bed. He tears off the girl's arm and replaces it with his own. Then he embraces her arm and kisses it.

The intent of *One Arm* will probably never be known, and Kawabata may not have had a single meaning in mind. He may have been under the influence of drugs. But one can read the story for its moments of uncanny perception. The techniques employed are those of Surrealism, a return by Kawabata to his earliest period.

After receiving the Nobel Prize in November 1968, Kawabata wrote almost nothing, though he made many false starts. He was lionized as the first Japanese to have received the prize, and a third set of his *Complete Works* was published. Mishima Yukio's suicide in November 1970 was especially painful to Kawabata, who, years before, had discovered the talents of the younger man.

On April 16, 1972, Kawabata went to an apartment overlooking the sea at Hayama where he was accustomed to writing manuscripts. He committed suicide by inhaling gas. There was no farewell note. Most Japanese

---

*Yasunari Kawabata, *One Arm*, in *House of the Sleeping Beauties and Other Stories*, trans. Edward G. Seidensticker (Tokyo: Kodansha International, 1969), p. 103.

were not surprised, finding his suicide hardly different from a natural death. Those who felt close to him, however, must have felt disappointed that not even the beauty that Kawabata had discovered in Japanese landscapes, in Japanese women, or in Japanese art had kept him from exploring the one realm that this perpetual traveler had never visited.

Mishima Yukio

(1925–1970)

Outside his own country Mishima Yukio is probably the most famous Japanese who ever lived. Europeans and Americans who would have difficulty naming even one Japanese emperor, politician, general, scientist, or poet are acquainted with Mishima's name, if not his works. In large part, of course, this is the result of his spectacular suicide, but even before this event he was the only Japanese chosen by *Esquire* magazine in its selection of one hundred leading figures of the world, and the only Japanese who appeared on internationally televised programs.

Mishima's death on November 25, 1970, came as a shock to the Japanese. Many were alarmed at what they feared might be a recrudescence of the right-wing nationalism that had prevailed in Japan before 1945. Once the initial shock had passed, critics published explanations of why Mishima had killed himself and why, if he was determined to die, he had chosen to commit *seppuku*, the ritual disembowelment. A few authors, probably imagining reasons that might drive themselves to suicide, opined that Mishima killed himself because he had discovered he no longer could write. The prime minister of Japan labeled Mishima's suicide an act of madness. Many other interpretations have since been published. My own, reduced to the simplest terms, is that his death was the logical culmination of a life consecrated to a particular kind of aesthetics.

Mishima's final compositions, a manifesto (*geki*) and two farewell poems to the world (*jisei*), portray himself as a rough-hewn soldier, so bitterly unhappy about the lamentable state of affairs prevailing in his country that he has chosen to offer his life by way of remonstration. Mishima directed that his posthumous name, the Buddhist name that would be inscribed on his tombstone, include the word *bu* for "martial." Perhaps he really felt indignation and even anguish over the failure of the Self-Defense Force—the Japanese army—to maintain order when leftist radicals demonstrated, but it is hard for me to suppress the thought that such acts were a kind of self-hypnosis, part of his efforts to convince himself that he was not so much a writer as a patriot.

In June 1970, on the night the security treaty with the United States came up for renewal, I was in a taxi with Mishima on our way to a restaurant. For ten years, ever since the demonstrations of 1960 against renewing the treaty, it had been widely predicted that the riots in 1970 would be on a much greater scale. Probably Mishima believed these predictions, and it may have been with the intention of defending the imperial palace against the rioters that he formed his tiny private army, the Shield Society. Of course, one hundred men could hardly prevent tens of thousands of demonstrators from breaking into the palace, but they could die, and that was Mishima's real object. But when our taxi passed the Diet buildings, there was no sign of demonstrators, only bored policemen carrying shields and clubs they would not use that night. This may have been when Mishima decided he would have to kill himself, now that there was no chance of being killed on the palace steps.

The last of his literary compositions was a *tanka* composed on November 23, 1970, two days before Mishima and the young men he had chosen to be the witnesses of his self-immolation set off for the headquarters of the Self-Defense Force:

chiru wo itou	Storm winds at night blow
yo ni mo hito ni mo	The message that to fall before
sakigakete	The world and before men
chiru koso hana to	By whom falling is dreaded
fuku sayo arashi	Is the mark of a flower.

This *tanka* is a pastiche of the language and imagery of the *jisei* poems composed by innumerable Japanese soldiers before their death. By "to fall," Mishima of course meant to die. Although other people dreaded the thought of death, by dying Mishima could prove he was a flower among men; the samurai, ready always to give up his life, is like the cherry blossoms, the quickest flower to fall.

Mishima composed another *tanka* earlier that year, in July, and this too served as a *jisei*:

masurao ga	For how many years
tabasamu tachi no	Has the warrior endured
saya naru ni	The rattling of
iku tose taete	The sword he wears at his side:
kyō no hatsushimo	The first fall of frost came today.

It is not clear what Mishima meant by "first frost" (*hatsushimo*), but the term was peculiar in a poem composed in July. Perhaps he anticipated, even four months earlier, his death in November when white frost would cover the ground.

These two *tanka* were the last he composed. They also were the first he had composed since 1942, when he was seventeen years old. For twenty-eight years he had not felt impelled to use the classic Japanese verse form as a medium to express his emotions, but he was determined to play to the full the role of the dying samurai, and one of the elements of that role was the farewell verse to the world. Because *jisei* were also composed by people who died of old age or from the complications of a bad cold, it is often difficult to tell from the poem alone the circumstances of the poet's death, but Mishima's *jisei* are somehow ominous. He tells us that up to now he has deliberately ignored the rattling of his broadsword, striving to suppress his anger, but his patience is exhausted, and he will let the sword have its own way.

It was probably shortly after composing his final *jisei* that Mishima wrote farewell letters to three old friends, including Ivan Morris and myself.

The opening sentence of the one I received was "When you read these words I shall be dead." Then, as if to lighten the mood created by this declaration, he recalled that I had often written his name not with the normal characters for Mishima Yukio but with facetiously chosen inauspicious characters that meant something like "Not yet dead demon, dim devil tail." I had done this by way of "revenge" for the funny characters he used when writing my name. Now my joke had acquired sinister overtones, as if I had been expecting his death all along. It was strange that Mishima recalled this bit of mischief on my part in what he knew would be his last letter to me, but this recollection may have seemed appropriate to the final actions of a samurai. In the letter he said that he had long wanted to die not as a writer but as a military man.

There was one thing in that letter (and also in the letter sent to Ivan Morris) that was definitely not in accordance with his chosen role. He had heard that American publishers were unwilling to publish works by dead foreign authors. This was not true, but somehow he had convinced himself of it, and he asked Ivan and me to do everything we could to ensure the publication of the translation of his final tetralogy, *The Sea of Fertility*. But why should a man, about to commit suicide in a most spectacular manner and resolved to die as a military man rather than as a writer, have cared whether or not his books were published in foreign translation? Obviously, he could never die only as a samurai; literature was too much a part of his makeup to be rejected.

Mishima's first major novel, *Confessions of a Mask* (*Kamen no kokuhaku*), published in 1949 when he was twenty-four, tells how he felt compelled to wear a mask before others. At first the mask may have put on by way of self-protection, as was true of Dazai Osamu, a novelist for whom Mishima always professed intense dislike. Dazai wrote that early in life he discovered how different he was from the people surrounding him and that the only way he could protect himself from the others was to wear a mask and pretend to be like them. His mask covered a face that probably wore an expression of self-pity. Mishima put on his mask for quite different reasons. His efforts were always directed not at concealing his real expression from the gaze of other people but at making his face into the mask he had chosen. He used the mask to subdue the sensitivity, timidity, and self-pity that Dazai carefully preserved behind his. Mishima was able to make the mask a living part of his flesh, and he died with it firmly in place. In the end, he may not even have been aware that he wore a mask, so much had its attitudes and his own coalesced.

One element shared by the mask—the simple, unaffected man of action—and Mishima the writer was the belief in the beauty of early death. As a high-school student at the Peers' School, Mishima was attracted especially to the novels and personality of Raymond Radiguet, the brilliant French author who died in 1923 at the age of twenty. Mishima remained fascinated with youth, and especially with youthful death, throughout his career as a writer. Unlike Doctor Faustus, who craved youth only after he had become old, Mishima yearned for youth even while he was still quite young—not eternal youth, but youth that ended with the dramatic suddenness of the fall of a cherry blossom. In 1966, when he was forty-one, he wrote, "Among my incurable convictions is the belief that the old are eternally ugly, the young eternally beautiful. The wisdom of the old is eternally murky, the actions of the young eternally transparent. The longer people live, the worse they become. Human life, in other words, is an upside-down process of decline and fall."

I cannot prove that Mishima was influenced by the fourteenth-century Buddhist priest Yoshida Kenkō, but their expression is strikingly similar. Kenkō wrote in Essays in Idleness (Tsurezure-gusa),

We cannot live forever in this world; why should we wait for ugliness to overtake us? The longer man lives, the more shame he endures. To die, at the latest, before one reaches forty, is the least unattractive. Once a man passes that age, he desires (with no sense of shame over his appearance) to mingle in the company of others. In his sunset years he dotes on his grandchildren and prays for long life so that he may see them prosper. His preoccupation with worldly desires grows ever deeper, and gradually he loses all sensitivity to the beauty of things, a lamentable state of affairs.

Kenkō, whose influence on the development of Japanese aesthetics was enormous, insisted on the importance of the perishability of things. Even Japanese who have never read *Essays in Idleness* can empathize with this belief, as we know from the special Japanese fondness for cherry blossoms. Cherry blossoms are lovely, it is true, but not so lovely as to eclipse totally the beauty of plum blossoms or peach blossoms. Even so, the Japanese plant cherry trees everywhere, even in parts of the country whose climate does not favor them, and they pay scant attention to plum or peach blossoms. Perhaps the greatest attraction of the cherry blossoms is not so much their intrinsic beauty as their perishability. Plum blossoms remain on the boughs for almost a month, and other fruit trees bear blossoms that last a week, but the cherry blossoms fall after a brief three days. Moreover, the Japanese cherry trees (unlike plum or peach trees) do not bear edible fruit; the Japanese plant these trees solely for their three days of glory.

I wonder if Mishima's often repeated insistence on the beauty of early death had similar origins. At the commemorative funeral service on the first anniversary of Mishima's death, the distinguished critic Yamamoto Kenkichi asked why Mishima had not taken to heart the writings of the great playwright of nō, Zeami, who had described the different "flower" appropriate to each stage of a man's life. Yamamoto was sure that if Mishima had not killed himself at the age of forty-five, his art would have blossomed in later life in ways not possible in a young man and that these works of his maturity would have added to the luster of his oeuvre. I doubt that Mishima would have agreed. Each sign of approaching old age— whether short-windedness when he raced around a track or even the realization that his tastes in food had changed and he now preferred traditional Japanese dishes—stirred in him regret that he had not been able to die young.

Mishima was given the perfect opportunity to die young during the war. He was called up for an army physical examination. He decided, apparently on the advice of his father, to undergo this examination in what was technically his permanent domicile, the family's ancestral home in Hiroshima Prefecture. In Tokyo, where he was born and had lived all his life, his undernourished physique would have passed unnoticed, but in Hiroshima, among the strapping young men from the farms, he would have looked frail to the point of debility. In addition, he happened to have a cold on the day of the examination, and when the inexperienced young doctor asked if he always had a fever and coughed so much, he nodded gravely. His cold was diagnosed as pleurisy, and he was sent home the same day, to his joy and relief. Some recent Japanese critics have interpreted Mishima's fascination with the military and with early death as a response to the humiliation he experienced at failing his medical test. I doubt this; if he had wished to be accepted for military service, all he would have had to do was to answer the doctor truthfully. But I think it quite likely that in his forties, he felt he had missed something by not having served in the army. He received permission to undergo training with the Self-Defense Force, and he clearly enjoyed the fraternal companionship. Surrounded by men half his age, Mishima shared their jokes and ate the same terrible food. If he felt any guilt over his wartime experiences, it was not because he had failed his medical test but because he had failed to die. The unit that he would have entered if he had passed the medical examination was not long afterward massacred in the Philippines.

The narrator of *Confessions of a Mask* exults in the thought of an early death, imagining that his scrawny, unattractive body will somehow, miraculously, attain the glory of the martyred St. Sebastian. I asked Mishima once if the schoolboy compositions included in *Confessions of a Mask* (including a prose poem on St. Sebastian) were actually written when he was a middle-school student, and he said they were; his fascination with the beautiful young man who dies transfixed by arrows began early. The narrator of the novel states that his first ejaculation was occasioned while looking at a reproduction of Guido Reni's painting of the martyrdom of St. Sebastian. Mishima touched on the death of St. Sebastian in his later works as well, although sometimes he referred instead to the similar instance of Adonis, the young god whose blood must be shed. This theme is particularly prominent in his works of the 1960s.

The heroes of Mishima's works are often men who die young or dream of a youthful death. The narrator of *Kinkakuji* (*The Temple of the Golden Pavilion* in Ivan Morris's translation) is a high-school student who yearns to perish together with the Kinkaku, a building he adores, in the wartime destruction of Japan. When the building escapes unscathed from the war, he has no choice but to destroy it himself, still with the hope of dying with it. The hero of *Runaway Horses* (*Homba*), a boy of the same age, is so enraged by the spiritual corruption of Japan that he kills a politician, an emblematic figure of all he detests, before turning his knife on himself. In the novel *Gogo no eikō*, translated as *The Sailor Who Fell from Grace with the Sea*, a sailor falls from grace with some boys who worshiped him because of his reluctance to die young in the manner of a true hero; they therefore preserve his glory by killing him.

Death and love were intertwined in Mishima's imagination. In 1961 he published *Patriotism* (*Yūkoku*), the first of several novellas and plays devoted to the ideals of the young officers or the 1960s. Mishima was fascinated by the unselfish idealism of these men who eagerly laid down their lives for the emperor. *Patriotism* is set at the time of the abortive coup of February 26, 1936. Lieutenant Takeyama, the hero, was not included in the coup because his friends were reluctant to involve a newly married man in a suicidal endeavor. But he resents having been excluded and decides he must kill himself in order to prove that he was no less ready than they to die for the emperor. His bride, aware of what it means to be the wife of a military man, does not attempt to dissuade him. Then, after he has committed *seppuku*, she plunges a dagger into her throat. Mishima did not intend their suicides to seem either pathetic or horrifying; on the contrary, he felt that Lieutenant Takeyama and his bride had achieved the greatest joy in life. Just before they kill themselves, they make love with the ardor of newlyweds and with delight in each other's bodies. They die, still young and beautiful, still deeply in love and absolutely secure in their beliefs.

Mishima himself took the part of Lieutenant Takeyama when the work was made into a film. The music played throughout was the *Liebestod* from *Tristan und Isolde*.

It was essential to Mishima's story that Lieutenant Takeyama kill himself by committing *seppuku*, the ritual disembowelment. Obviously, an overdose of sleeping pills or a leap from the roof of a building would not have made a satisfactory ending to the story. But this *seppuku* did not have the usual sense of proving, by exposing one's entrails, that one is free of any taint of guilt, nor was it a punishment imposed from above on a samurai who had disobeyed an order. Nor was Lieutenant Takeyama following his master—the emperor—in death. It was not even a gesture of remonstrance, urging the government to return to the path of virtue. It was a love-death, the exaltation of the lovers leading to the supreme moment when love and death are one.

The form of the deaths was traditional, just as the thinking of both Lieutenant Takeyama and his bride was traditional. Lieutenant Takeyama would have been ready to die for the emperor on the battlefield without an instant of hesitation or uncertainty. His bride was a traditional Japanese wife, mild and gentle, who did not question her husband's decision but who had the strength of purpose to drive a dagger into her throat. This was the Japan that fascinated Mishima, the Japan that formed the foundation of his aesthetic.

In 1967 Mishima published *Introduction to* Hagakure (*Hagakure nyū-mon*). *Hagakure* is a book of reflections, completed in 1716, by a samurai named Yamamoto Tsunetomo. The work opens with a famous statement: *Bushidō to iu wa, shinu koto to mitsuketari*. A free translation would be "Bushidō—the way of the warrior—consists in discovering when to die." Mishima said of this work that it was the matrix of his entire literary production and the source of his vitality as a writer. This was surely an overstatement, but we know that he read *Hagakure* during the war years and that its ideals—those of the samurai—never left him, even when he shirked military duty.

Mishima's emperor-worship, probably the most controversial aspect of his thought, seems to have stemmed from the same source. His emperor-worship was not directed at Hirohito, the reigning emperor throughout Mishima's life. He even would mimic the emperor at a garden party, saying *Aa, sō* in response to every word he heard. In Mishima's story "The Voices of the Heroic Dead" (Eirei no koe), the ghosts of the leaders of the February 26 incident and the *kamikaze* pilots of 1945 bitterly reproach the emperor for having betrayed them by declaring that he was not a god. Those who died in the name of the emperor knew, of course, that he was a human being with ordinary human weaknesses, but they were sure that in his capacity as emperor, he was a god. If he had supported the young officers who participated in the February 26 incident and especially if he had ordered them to commit suicide, he would have behaved like a god and not like a mere ruler surrounded by aged and corrupt politicians. When the emperor declared that he was not a god less than a year after the *kamikaze* pilots had joyfully died with his name on their lips, he made their sacrifice a pitiable, meaningless gesture.

Mishima once declared that he believed in the infallibility of the emperor. This, of course, did not refer to the emperor in his human capacities, any more than a belief in papal infallibility implies unconditional acceptance of the pope's views on modern art. Rather, in his capacity as a god, the emperor is the incarnation of Japanese tradition, the unique repository of the experience of the Japanese people. To protect the emperor was, for Mishima, to protect Japan itself. It would be a mistake to identify these political views with the Japanese right wing. Especially in his novel *Runaway Horses*, Mishima demonstrated his awareness of the sinister motives of professional supporters of right-wing causes. He was sure that only the purity of the young, the readiness of the young to die for their beliefs, could save Japanese culture from disintegration under the double threat of greed—the merciless hacking away of Japan's landscapes—and Westernization—the superficial adoption of foreign things and manners because they are foreign.

Mishima's love of tradition developed into an unchanging element in his aesthetics. His insistence on tradition accounts for his retention of the

traditional orthography, although almost every other writer of his generation adopted the spelling reforms promulgated after the end of the war in
1945. He had nothing but scorn for writers (like Dazai) who could not write
the language appropriate to the upper classes. He had a very clear idea of
what traditional etiquette involved and did not readily forgive anyone who
transgressed. But perhaps the respect in which he differed most conspicuously from other writers of his generation was his knowledge of Japanese
classical literature and his use of this literature in his own works.

It is recorded that Abe Kōbō, when asked what traditional Japanese
literature had contributed to his writings, responded, "Nothing." Perhaps
he was joking or was hoping merely to surprise his interlocutor. Mishima
might have answered, "Everything," although that too would have been
misleading. All the same, he thought of himself as a classical writer and
again and again turned to the classics of both Japan and the West for
inspiration or at least a sounding board on which to test his own ideas. The
most obvious of his borrowings from Japanese classical literature are his
modern nō plays in which he borrowed the themes of fifteenth-century
plays, though he set them in contemporary Japan—in a couturier's establishment, a law firm, a psychoanalyst's office, and so on. Implicit in these
borrowings was the belief that the themes treated in the old plays still had
relevance today, as well as his belief that the freedom with which the nō
playwright used time and space could enrich the modern stage. He also
wrote plays based on the Greek tragedies; his respect for Japanese tradition
did not imply a rejection of non-Japanese traditions.

Mishima's plays include versions of two plays by Euripides, *Medea* and
Herakles, and an extraordinary work for the Bunraku puppet theater based
on Racine's *Phèdre*. In such instances, the resulting play was entirely Japanese. *The Fall of the House of Suzaku* (*Suzaku-ke no metsubō*), the play
based on *Herakles*, is about an aristocratic family in Tokyo during and after
the bombings of 1945. I think it unlikely that anyone seeing the play without
prior knowledge that it was based on *Herakles* would guess its origins, so
completely does it suit particular Japanese circumstances.

Perhaps Mishima's most conspicuous borrowing from the West is the plot of the novel *The Sound of Waves* (*Shiosai*). Although most readers find it typically Japanese in its theme and expression, it is fairly closely based on the ancient Greek romance *Daphnis and Chloë*. Mishima conscientiously followed the plot of the original, although he had no choice but to change the shepherd and shepherdess of the Greek story into a fisherboy and fishergirl, there being no sheep in Japan. Mishima thought of *The Sound of Waves* as being essentially an exercise in stylistics, giving new life to the familiar boy-meets-girl story by the use of artfully chosen details of life on an island off the Ise coast.

The Sound of Waves also represented a kind of protest against the appearance and attitudes prevalent among Japanese intellectuals of that time. One day in 1955, while visiting an exhibition of photographs in Tokyo, Mishima happened to notice the face of a man near him. Suddenly, he related, "his ugliness infuriated me. I thought, 'What an ugly thing an intellectual face is! What an unseemly spectacle an intellectual human being makes!'" This revelation, which long had been germinating, made him hate the sensitivity within himself, the kind of sensitivity that so easily expressed itself in the martyred look of the intellectual. Mishima decided he must do something drastic about his own appearance, and soon afterward he began to lift weights, with such vigor and persistence that he was eventually able to create, from the most unpromising material, a highly muscular torso.

Mishima's attraction to Greece, which began with a brief visit in 1952, remained with him for the rest of his life, and the influence can be detected in many works. Mishima did not feel that this influence conflicted in any way with his love of Japanese tradition. It meant sunlit landscapes, as opposed to the shadows more commonly favored by Japanese writers. It probably also meant the uncomplicated mind of the Greek hero, a quality shared by the fisherboy of *The Sound of Waves* and also by the various young army officers he portrayed, men untroubled by self-doubt.

Mishima was a classical writer not only in his love of the classics of Japan and the West, but also in his use of many of their conventions.

Perhaps his best play is *Madame de Sade* (*Sado kōshaku fujin*, 1965), in which he adopted the conventions of the plays of Racine — a single setting; a limited number of characters, each of whom represents a specific quality; the absence of overt action; and a reliance on *tirades*, long recitations by the characters describing events and emotions. If one sees this play performed in translation — particularly in French translation — one is likely to forget that it was written by a Japanese, but there is nothing un-Japanese about it; in fact, the long-suffering Madame de Sade may seem more Japanese than French. But the point is surely not the degree of influence Mishima received from European literature but how successful he was in making it a part of himself and turning the received influence into new creations of artistic value.

Mishima's classicism is revealed also in his borrowings from conspicuously unclassical sources. Mishima modeled his novel *The Blue Period* (*Ao no jidai*), written in 1950, on actual events as reported in the press. The novel was faithful to the facts, telling about a Tokyo University student who lent money at usurious rates of interest, was caught, and finally committed suicide. The novel *After the Banquet* (*Utage no ato*, 1960) was so close to the facts of an unsuccessful campaign for the governorship of Tokyo that Mishima was sued for invasion of privacy and lost the case. The veteran politician Arita Hachirō, formerly a conservative, had become a socialist after the war and in 1959 ran for the post of governor of Tokyo. Not long before he began his campaign, he married the proprietress of the Hannya-en, a fashionable restaurant in Tokyo known for its magnificent garden. The new Mrs. Arita, a woman in her fifties, threw herself and her financial resources into the campaign, but disclosures about her past were instrumental in bringing about Arita's defeat in the election. The background, known to many of the first readers of the novel, lent piquance to its revelations, real or invented.

Mishima wrote as a classicist, using materials that were familiar to his readers and assuming that they knew the conclusion of his story even before they opened the book; but he imbued the familiar materials, whether real or fictitious, with his personality as an artist. The finest example of this kind of classicism was his novel *Kinkakuji*, the story of the man who burned the celebrated temple.

The burning of the Kinkaku came as a shock not only to the people in the city of Kyoto but also to everyone who admired the traditional culture of Japan. The temple as a whole had been erected at the beginning of the fifteenth century by the shogun Ashikaga Yoshimitsu on the site of a villa. Most of the temple buildings were destroyed during the warfare of the sixteenth century, but the Kinkaku had miraculously survived the fires. It was because of the Kinkakuji and the other famous temples in Kyoto that the city escaped bombing by American airplanes during the Pacific War. This made it seem all the more deplorable when, five years after the war ended, on July 1, 1950, a priest of the temple set fire to the Kinkaku and reduced it to ashes.

The motives that led the priest, Hayashi Yōken, to commit his act of arson remain unclear. He stated at his trial that it was to protest against the commercialization of Buddhism (the temple was a celebrated tourist attraction), but he may have been directly inspired by nothing more significant than pique over having been given a worn garment when he asked the superior of the temple for an overcoat. Neither the trial records nor the remembrances of people who knew Hayashi suggest that there were deep-reaching motives for his crime, but Mishima found in Hayashi the hero he needed for a philosophical novel. He read the newspaper reports and the trial records and also visited Hayashi in his cell. He told me, however, that the visit had added nothing to what he previously had known.

Mishima's use of the facts was confined to the relatively few instances when they were necessary for the framework of his book. His hero, called Mizoguchi, came, like Hayashi, from a desolate village on the Japan Sea coast, where his father was the priest of a small Zen temple. By all accounts (including his own testimony at the trial), Hayashi was painfully aware of his ugliness, and he suffered also from a paralyzing stutter that made him inarticulate. Mishima adopted these physical traits for his hero. He may have been attracted by the irony that a monument of surpassing beauty, which had withstood the ravages of warfare and the passage of the centuries, was destroyed by so unattractive and so unmemorable a man.

The conclusion of the novel—the burning of the Kinkaku—was surely known to all Japanese readers before they looked at Mishima's book. Mishima seems to have relished the problem of giving new life to a well-known story, transforming the facts, as he had transformed the story of *Daphnis and Chloë*, by giving them new meaning. Mishima consciously wrote a philosophical novel. He realized, of course, that the complicated ideas voiced by his characters, notably Mizoguchi's disagreeable classmate Kashiwagi, might put off readers who sought nothing more from a novel than entertainment, but he took the risk, and he was brilliantly successful. Despite the difficulties involved, in both the *kōan*, or Zen riddles, that appear at strategic moments in the narration and Mizoguchi's inexplicable love–hate relationship with beauty, the book was a popular success and was made into a film and later into an opera. Many readers probably could not grasp all the intended implications of the dialogue, but the story moves with relentless momentum toward the known conclusion—the burning of the Kinkaku—and this no doubt carried along even the least philosophically minded.

Kinkakuji is a difficult book. The easiest way of interpreting it is perhaps the one adopted by the American writer who first introduced the translation of the novel: she discussed it in terms of "Mizoguchi's sick mind" and "his mad career through a series of nihilistic, self-destructive actions." As an objective criticism of the young man's behavior, this opinion can hardly be disputed, but surely this was not Mishima's intention. It is essential that the reader sympathize with Mizoguchi even when he performs socially unacceptable actions and even when he commits the unforgivable crime of destroying one of the chief monuments of Japanese architecture. The novel as a whole is a tour de force: it not only persuades the readers, against their moral judgment, that it was necessary for Mizoguchi to commit the crime but makes them rejoice when the young man at last destroys the obstacle to his happiness.

Early in the novel Mizoguchi tells us:

It is no exaggeration to say that the first real problem I faced in my life was that of beauty. My father was only a simple country priest, deficient in vocabulary, and he taught me that "there is nothing on earth so beautiful as the Golden Temple." At the thought that beauty should already have come into the world unknown to me, I could not help feeling a certain uneasiness and irritation. If beauty really did exist there, it meant that my own existence was a thing estranged from beauty.*

It is difficult, perhaps impossible, to accept these words as expressing what a badly educated boy living in a remote part of the country would really have thought. It is much less difficult, however, to imagine Mishima adopting this unlikely persona and attributing to Mizoguchi what he himself had felt, identifying with him at each step leading to the final decision to set fire to the Kinkaku.

When Mizoguchi first sees the building, he is disappointed: the reality cannot live up to his father's praise. But after he is accepted as an acolyte and comes to live in the temple, the building takes possession of him, and he addresses it in these terms:

"Finally I have come to live beside you, Golden Temple!" I whispered in my heart, and for a while I stopped sweeping the leaves. "It doesn't have to be at once, but please make friends with me sometime and reveal your secret to me. I feel that your beauty is something that I am very close to seeing and yet cannot see. Please let me see the real Golden Temple more clearly than I can see the image of you in my

---

*Yukio Mishima, *The Temple of the Golden Pavilion*, trans. Ivan Morris (New York: Vintage, 1994), p. 21.

mind. And furthermore, if you are indeed so beautiful that nothing in this world can compare with you, please tell me why you are so beautiful, why it is necessary for you to be so beautiful."*

This is surely more the prayer of the young Mishima than of Mizoguchi, but it is not necessary to separate the two. Mishima was able to identify fully with his creation. When Mizoguchi holds a girl in his arms, the absolute beauty of the temple appears before his eyes, preventing him from making love to the girl, who is no more than ordinarily beautiful. After reading the novel, friends of Mishima teased him with the implausibility of any man resisting natural desires under such circumstances, regardless of his conception of beauty; but Mishima told me that he had actually had this experience. The successful transference of the emotional and aesthetic reactions of a highly educated and sensitive man to a youth who might uncharitably be called a clod makes it possible for the reader to accept as genuine Mizoguchi's thoughts and actions, despite the evidence that he is in no way capable of formulating so complicated an appreciation of beauty.

The problem of the existence of beauty preoccupies Mizoguchi, who comes to suppose that his conception of beauty must itself be responsible for his ugliness. Once he has made this discovery, his actions become inevitable. He must destroy his enemy; as the incarnation of beauty, the Kinkaku must be destroyed by the man who loves it most.

The Kinkakuji is a Zen temple. Mishima's family ties were also with Zen Buddhism, but there was probably no special significance in this fact. The parishioners of a Zen temple, like most other Buddhists today, normally have little to do with the temple with which they are affiliated except immediately after there has been a death in the family.

All the same, Zen Buddhism is present throughout the novel, from the

---

*Ibid., p. 36.

first mention by Mizoguchi's father of the wondrous beauty of the Kinkaku until the moment when, as he watches the building being consumed in the flames, Mizoguchi decides to go on living. One Zen *kōan* appears in the novel three times, each time given a different interpretation. On August 15, 1945, the day when the emperor announced the unconditional surrender of Japan, the superior of the Kinkakuji recounted the *kōan* known as "Nansen Kills a Cat." This is the story of a kitten that has become the object of contention between the east and west halls of a temple in China. The chief priest, Nansen, catches the kitten and says if anyone can give reason why he should not kill it, he will spare its life. No one speaks up, so Nansen kills the kitten. Later, when his chief disciple, Jōshū, returns to the temple and learns what has happened in his absence, he removes his shoes and puts them on his head. Seeing this, Nansen laments that Jōshū was not present when he asked for reasons why he should spare the kitten; if he had been there, the kitten would have been saved.

Of the three explanations of the *kōan* given by characters in the novel, the second, by Kashiwagi, Mizoguchi's evil friend, emphasizes the beauty of the kitten that Nansen killed; indeed, it was because of its beauty that dissension had arisen between the two halls. Although Kashiwagi does not usually speak for Mishima, in this instance his explanation of the problem of beauty seems close to Mishima's own:

> Beauty . . . is like a decayed tooth. It rubs against one's tongue, it hangs there, hurting one, insisting on its own existence. Finally it gets so that one cannot stand the pain and one goes to the dentist to have the tooth extracted. . . . To have killed the kitten, therefore, seemed just like having extracted a painful decayed tooth, like having gouged out beauty. Yet it was uncertain whether or not this had really been a final solution. The root of the beauty had not been severed, and even though the kitten was dead, the kitten's beauty might very well still be alive. And so, you see, it was in order to satirize the glibness of this solution that Jōshū put those shoes on his head. He knew, so to speak, that there

was no possible solution other than enduring the pain of the decayed tooth.*

This and the other explanations of the *kōan* are not easy to follow, and the reader who is unwilling to go on with the novel until he is satisfied that he knows exactly what the *kōan* means risks losing track of the story. Mishima was aware of this danger inherent in a philosophical novel but accepted it, making the burning of the temple a *kōan* of his own.

Mishima continued writing almost up to the day of his spectacular suicide on November 25, 1970. He himself believed that his best work, the repository of all that he had learned as a novelist, was in the final tetralogy, *The Sea of Fertility*. This is in every respect a major work. It seems even to trace allegorically the moods of Japanese literature from the time of *The Tale of Genji* to the present (and even the future). My favorite is the first volume, *Spring Snow* (*Haru no yuki*), written in a manner evocative of the Heian romances, even though it treats Japan of the twentieth century. Mishima always rejected the lyricism that would have come so easily to him, but in this novel it flowers, albeit without letting us forget that he wrote it. The second volume, *Runaway Horses* (*Homba*), represents the culmination of Mishima's fascination with the young warrior, the hero who selflessly kills for an ideal and dies. The third volume, *The Temple of Dawn* (*Akatsuki no tera*), is set partly in Thailand, partly in postwar Japan. The emphasis here is on Buddhism, which gave reviewers in Japan, who alleged ignorance of religion, a good excuse for not discussing a work by the increasingly controversial Mishima. This novel is somewhat awkwardly divided between two different worlds, as Mishima himself recognized, but he was attempting to trace what lay behind the religious beliefs of the Japanese. It is difficult to think of any other Japanese novelist who would

---

*Ibid., p. 144.

have attempted a work on the grandiose scale of these three novels. Unfortunately, the final volume of the tetralogy, *The Decay of the Angel* *(Tennin Gosui)*, is marred by signs of haste and even carelessness, perhaps because Mishima, knowing exactly the day on which he would die, had difficulty concentrating on the work at hand.

Mishima chose for his suicide the day of the month on which he regularly delivered chapters of his novel to the magazine in which it was being serialized. On this occasion, the editor telephoned to ask, as a special favor, that he give her the manuscript one day earlier. He refused, saying it would not be complete. This was not true. That summer he had put in my hands the manuscript of the final chapter. He told me he had written it "in one breath." I did not ask to read the manuscript, supposing that without knowing what had preceded, I would be unable to understand the last chapter. But even though it had been written in August, it was essential to Mishima that he die on the day he completed his masterpiece. He dated the last page November 25.

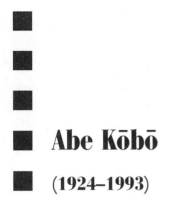

Abe Kōbō

(1924–1993)

I first met Abe Kōbō in the autumn of 1964. He had come to New York in connection with the publication by Knopf of the English translation of his novel *The Woman in the Dunes* (*Suna no onna*). I forget why he decided to visit Columbia University, but I distinctly remember his arrival in 407 Kent Hall. He was accompanied by Teshigahara Hiroshi, the director of the celebrated film made from this novel, which had won the Grand Prize at the Cannes Film Festival that year. With them came a young Japanese woman. I confess that I was rather miffed when I was informed that the young woman was their interpreter, and in order to demonstrate that I had no need of an interpreter, I studiously avoided even looking at her. It was only years later that I learned that she was Ono Yōko.

It was about lunchtime, so I invited all three of my visitors to a Chinese restaurant on 110th Street. I was suffering from jet lag, having only recently returned from Japan, and I suppose that I may have acted in a somewhat somnolent manner. Abe, a graduate of the medical school of Tokyo University, observed me carefully and concluded from my manner of walking that I was a drug addict, as he later informed me. All in all, one could hardly say that our first meeting had been a success.

Three years later, in the spring of 1967 while I was on sabbatical leave in Japan, Ōe Kenzaburō, with whom I had become friendly, suggested that we invite Abe to join us for dinner. I welcomed the suggestion, but Abe evidently did not. He went instead to a prizefight. It was later explained to me that Abe was a devoted fan of Fighting Harada, who had a match that night, but Ōe and I, watching the television of the bout, searched in vain for Abe—or anyone at all wearing dark-rimmed glasses—among the spectators. It seemed likely that the dismal impression I had created on Abe in New York, even more than devotion to Fighting Harada, accounted for his unwillingness to dine with us. It took Ōe considerable time and effort to overcome Abe's resistance to meeting me again, but once it happened, with the aid of a considerable amount of liquor, we became friends and remained close until his death in 1993.

I did not know Abe's writings very well at this time. The first of his works I read was *The Woman in the Dunes* in the fine translation by Dale Saunders. Later, I read in Japanese Abe's novel *The Face of Another* (*Tanin no kao*) and some stories of the 1960s. This was a period of extraordinary activity for Abe. For example, in 1964, the year of our disastrous first meeting, he was publishing serially two major novels simultaneously in different magazines. He also published a collection of short stories and a collection of essays, and he won a prize for the best radio drama of the year.

Two years earlier, in 1962, Abe had been expelled from the Communist Party. In fact, his former membership in the party had made it difficult for him to obtain an American visa in 1964, and it was finally issued only with severe restrictions on where he might travel and how long he might stay. Well after his books had made it clear that he had rejected Communist ideology and even after he had become persona non grata in Soviet Russia, he continued to experience the same hampering restrictions when visiting America. As far as I could tell, however, this seems not to have inspired in him the kind of anti-Americanism that was so prevalent in Japan, especially during the Vietnam War.

Abe was a maverick, incapable of aligning himself for long with any political movement or writing works in accordance with doctrinal lines. His independence and breadth of vision were often attributed by Japanese—who tend to emphasize geographical considerations as determining factors in a man's life—to his having grown up in Manchuria rather than in the insular world of Japan.

Abe was born in Tokyo in 1924. At the time his father, a medical doctor, was a professor at the Medical University of Manchuria (Manshū ika daigaku) but was temporarily in Tokyo doing research. The family moved to Mukden (Shen-yang) in the following year, and Abe spent his childhood there, attending Japanese schools. Although such schools were products of the Japanese occupation of Manchuria and signified the Japanese intention of remaining there permanently, the official line taught to the pupils was not that the Japanese were superior to the other inhabitants but that the five constituent peoples—Japanese, Chinese, Manchus, Mongols, and Russians—must live on terms of equality and harmony. As a boy Abe believed in this ideal, although he also must have been aware that other Japanese, enjoying their privileged position, accepted as a matter of course their predominant role in the new country. Even though Abe seemed to be permanently domiciled in Manchuria, he never forgot that he was Japanese. I recall Abe saying that boys in his school wore gloves in winter to distinguish themselves from the Chinese boys who wore mittens, even though mittens were much warmer.

But such awareness of the distinction between the Japanese and the other peoples of Manchuria was probably less important to Abe than what he unconsciously absorbed from the place. If he did not become a Manchurian, he was quite unlike a typical Japanese schoolboy. The textbooks he read in school, intended for children in Japan, contained such sentences as "In our country, the streams are pellucidly clear and the mountains are green." But the streams in Manchuria were few and likely to be muddied, and there were no mountains in sight, only immense, dusty plains merging imperceptibly into the desert. The contradiction between the textbook descriptions of "our country" and the visible reality of sand dunes behind the school building made the boy question the veracity of the textbooks. It inspired contradictory feelings: a yearning for Japan but also a sense of alienation from Japan. In later years, when he was actually living in Japan, such feelings kept him from identifying himself with Japanese landscapes. He told me once that he never could understand why Japanese were so fond of the ocean. More important, he developed a suspicion and even a hatred of manifestations of love of the soil—any soil—an emotion he came to associate with fascism.

In Abe's novel *The Woman in the Dunes*, the hero, a collector of rare insects that live in the dunes, finds himself as dusk comes on without a place to spend the night. He visits the village cooperative and asks their help. He notices a placard on the wall: "The Spirit of Love for One's Home-Place" (*aikyō seishin*). Later, he comes to understand that attachment to the soil, love of home-place, accounted for the villagers' determination to remain in the bleak dunes, eternally shoveling sand. The man appears just at a time when the villagers are in need of another hand to help shovel the sand. They lead him to a house buried in the dunes whose owner, a woman, welcomes him. Gradually he realizes that he is a prisoner, given enough to eat and provided with a woman, but compelled to keep shoveling the sand. Late in the novel the man, whose various attempts to escape have been frustrated, asks the woman why people go on living in such a place. She says it is because of the sand:

"The sand?" The man clamped his teeth together, rolling his head. "What good is the sand? Outside of giving you a hard time, it doesn't bring in a penny."

[The woman answers,] "Yes, it does. They sell it."

"You sell it? Who do you sell such stuff to?"

"Well, to construction companies and places like that. They mix it with concrete . . ."

"Don't be silly. It'd be a fine mess if you mixed this sand with cement—it's got too much salt in it. In the first place, it's probably against the law or at least against construction regulations . . ."

"Of course, they sell it secretly. They cut the hauling charges in half too . . ."

"That's too crazy! Even if it was free, that wouldn't make it right when buildings and dams start to collapse, would it?"

The woman suddenly interrupted him with accusing eyes. She

spoke coldly, looking at his chest, and her attitude was completely different.

"Why should we worry about what happens to other people?"*

The woman is elsewhere portrayed as a sympathetic though very nearly mute character, but in this one scene she reveals her love of the soil, the place where (she says) the bones of her child are buried, so strong that she is indifferent to whether or not the sand causes people to die in other places. Abe, who had two homelands—Manchuria and Japan—was attached to neither. I can hardly imagine him feeling either nostalgia or local pride, but he never forgot Manchuria, his lost homeland. He did not describe his life in Manchuria in the kind of first-person novel that is typical of twentieth-century Japanese literature, but his early writings evoked experiences on the continent, and it is probably no coincidence that the novel that established his reputation, *The Woman in the Dunes*, describes the part of Japan that most resembles the windswept dunes of Manchuria.

Abe left Manchuria in 1940 (when he was sixteen) in order to study at the Seijō High School in Tokyo. At school he excelled, especially at mathematics. He told me once, not long after he had attended a high-school reunion, that his classmates remembered him as a mathematical genius. His knowledge of science was also remarkable. Some years before his death, he appeared on a television program with an eminent physicist who, assuming that a novelist would have trouble understanding the terminology of modern physics, attempted to make things easier by simplifying his expression. To his astonishment, Abe brushed away the explanations with such assurance as to make the physicist look foolish.

Perhaps Abe inherited his fondness for science from his father; if so, per-

---

*Kōbō Abe, *The Woman in the Dunes*, trans. E. Dale Saunders (New York: Vintage, 1991), pp. 222–23 (slightly modified).

haps he inherited his love of literature from his mother, an unusually well educated woman for the time, who had taught Japanese classical literature and had even published a novel. The house in Mukden was full of books, and Abe was an omnivorous reader, especially translations of foreign literature.

One of the mysteries of this mysterious man was his inability to learn foreign languages. He told me once that at the age of fifteen he had qualified as an interpreter of Chinese, but I never heard him utter a word of Chinese, and I doubt that he remembered anything of the language. He was a genius at forgetting languages, both the Chinese and the English he had studied from middle-school days onward and the German he later studied as a requirement for entry into medical school. When Abe was in America, the kind of people who assume that every intelligent foreigner must surely know English frequently addressed Abe in English. If I informed them that he did not understand, they would snap back, "Of course he understands. You can see it in his eyes." Unfortunately, he did not understand, not even simple phrases, but he always looked intelligent.

The opposite face of Abe's inability to learn foreign languages was his extraordinary interest in the Japanese language. Most writers, of course, take pride in their ability to manipulate their native language and are all too ready to point out stylistic flaws in the works of their contemporaries. Mishima, in particular, was contemptuous of writers who failed to make the characters in their novels or plays speak the kind of Japanese appropriate to their class. But most writers, whether they insist on maintaining the purity of the Japanese language or advocate (under foreign influence) a greater use of relative clauses, take the language for granted and do not stop to think why they speak and write it as they do.

Especially in the years immediately before his death, Abe became preoccupied with the origins of the Japanese language. Some linguists confidently assign Japanese a place among the Altaic languages (which include Korean and Mongolian). Others have pointed out grammatical similarities between Japanese and the languages of southern India. Others still have attempted to trace the common origins of Japanese and the Ainu language.

Abe did not accept any of these theories. He read widely in linguistics, particularly studies of creoles—languages that have come into being spontaneously from combinations of existing languages but are not in a direct parent–child relation to any one language or group of languages. Abe was particularly interested in the creoles of Guyana and Hawaii as possible paradigms for the creation of the Japanese language.

Abe contributed funds to the research of Dr. Tsunoda Tadanobu, a specialist in the mechanics of hearing, who was studying the way in which the two halves of the brain process sounds. Tsunoda tried out on many people—including ordinary Japanese, persons of Japanese ancestry who had learned some other language first, and persons of non-Japanese ancestry who had learned Japanese from infancy—a test he had devised. He discovered that persons whose mother tongue was Japanese, regardless of their ancestry, all showed the same reactions to speech, humming, animal cries, music, miscellaneous noises, and so on. For example, they heard human speech and bird cries with the same hemisphere of the brain, but persons whose first language was not Japanese processed only human speech with that hemisphere of the brain. Abe was excited by what he took for a revelation of the fundamental nature of the Japanese language and even cited it jestingly to explain why he disliked opera so much. Many scholars subsequently denounced Tsunoda as a charlatan because he was the only person who could successfully perform the experiments; still others (mainly non-Japanese) considered the experiments to be deplorable examples of the Japanese tendency to emphasize their uniqueness. Tsunoda finally grew tired of the attacks and gave up his testing, despite Abe's encouragement.

Abe's special interest in the Japanese language may have originated in childhood perceptions of the differences between Japanese and Chinese, or it may have been his way of explaining to himself why he simply couldn't learn foreign languages. (He always showed distrust of Japanese who could speak another language fluently.) In any case, as an author, language was of extreme importance to him, and he expressed annoyance when his works were labeled by critics as "novels of ideas," as if his style—his use of language—were of only minor importance.

Abe was in Tokyo during most of the war years. I remember particularly his account of the first, small-scale American air raid in 1942. He told me how the boys at his high school excitedly gathered around the windows and cheered. I don't really believe this. I have trouble also believing, according to Abe, that the principal of the Seijō High School, a liberal who hated the militarists, was so filled with animosity for Takamura Kōtarō, a poet known for his belligerence, that he was incapable of speaking when he had to introduce the poet to the students. Abe, a writer of fiction, may have had trouble at times distinguishing between what actually had happened and what might have happened if other people were more like himself.

Abe's views of the truth were always entertaining. I remember, for example, his account of the difficulty he encountered in leaving Czechoslovakia because, at a village near the Austrian border, his passage was blocked by a gypsy woman who declared that she intended to make him her husband. Or, to give a less amusing instance, he related that while in Norway, a man deliberately bumped into him in a restaurant and said something insulting, supposing that he was a Vietnamese refugee. In view of Abe's inability to speak any foreign language, his interpretation of what the gypsy woman or the Norwegian man actually said could only be intuitive, not factual. But there were enough improbable occurrences in Abe's life to make almost any story he told seem plausible.

Abe entered the Tokyo University Medical School in 1943, at the age of nineteen. This gave him temporary exemption from the draft, but in the following year his unsatisfactory scholastic performance endangered the exemption. When the time came to take a medical examination to determine whether or not he was fit for military service, he, with the help of a friend, forged a medical certificate stating that he was suffering from tuberculosis.

The ruse succeeded. Abe was pronounced unfit for military duty and made his way back to Mukden in 1944. At first he helped his father with his medical practice, but in August 1945, just before the end of the war, a typhus epidemic swept Manchuria and the father caught the sickness and died. Abe remained in Mukden. To support himself, he invented a new brand of soda pop that was so successful that he was soon rolling in money. He did not trust the banks, so he stuffed the banknotes into the shutter boxes of his house. He was unable to return to Japan until the end of 1946 when he and others were repatriated aboard an American landing craft. His experiences during this journey provided the background for his first full-length novel, *Animals Head for Home* (*Kemonotachi wa kokyō wo mezasu*).

Other experiences in Manchuria directly or indirectly colored Abe's future writings. One came as a particular shock and affected not only his writings but also his outlook on life: it was seeing the lawless behavior of the Japanese troops in Mukden after the surrender. He felt such disgust on witnessing the crimes perpetrated by Japanese soldiers on Japanese civilians as to make him wish to renounce his identity as a Japanese. This disgust further developed into a hatred of any form of nationalism or of the belief that one "belonged" to a nation. In later years he was sometimes accused of being a rootless cosmopolite, but he accepted the charge. I once asked him why he so seldom gave names to the characters in his novels or plays. (They are called instead "the mother," "the boxer," "the fiancée," or simply, as in *The Woman in the Dunes*, "the man" and "the woman"). He said it was because it made things more difficult if he gave them names. He did not elaborate, but I wonder if he was not reluctant to confine his characters within the limitations of being Japanese—or any other nationality. He asked that when his plays were staged abroad, there be no suggestion of their Japanese origins.

Abe's internationalism was expressed politically by his decision to join the Communist Party, probably in 1949. As a high-school student, he had been attracted by socialism, but now he was less interested in socialist economics than in a political stance that would favor a removal of the barriers of nationalism that separate country and country or people and people.

After his return to Japan from China in 1946, Abe lived in great poverty.

Even if he had been able to take with him his fortune in Manchurian currency, it would have been worthless. For a time he lived in the house of a *yakuza* (gangster) boss who was so impressed by the young man from Manchuria that he wished to make him his successor. (This may be another example of Abe as mythmaker.) Later on, he lived in a crude shelter he had fashioned from loose timbers lying around a bombed site. Photographs of Abe taken at this time suggest that he did not eat very often. He told me once that he hadn't enough money to buy a new pair of glasses after he accidentally broke the ones he was wearing. When he went to the movies, he would take the largest pieces of the broken lenses and hold them in front of his eyes. This way of life may have contributed to his indifferent performance at medical school. He graduated in 1948 but was given his degree only on condition that he never practice medicine; his lack of enthusiasm for medicine, reflected in his poor grades, had evidently been recognized by his professors.

The possession of a medical degree may have pleased Abe, but because he was unable to practice, the degree brought in no income. In any case, by this time Abe had become increasingly involved with literature, especially of the avant-garde. In 1947 he had published privately a mimeographed pamphlet entitled *Collection of Anonymous Poems* (*Mumei shishū*). He and his wife (they married earlier that year) took a stack of these pamphlets to Hokkaido, where he had relatives. They bought one-way tickets, expecting that the relatives would buy enough copies at least to pay for the return train fare, but this assumption was wrong—they sold hardly a copy. (Today, this book is one of the rarest works of modern Japanese works of literature.) The poems, influenced by Rilke (whom he read in translation), are not easy to understand. This is the opening of "Fruit of the Apple," which he dedicated to his wife:

> Perhaps you too have brought forth a life
> Inside the fruit of the apple.
> Perhaps you have ripened a certain joy,
> Multiplying again and again shadows that pass over

The cheek, still green on one side.
I accepted it quietly in both hands,
And, for a long time, still vacant,
Trembled with the premonition I sustained
Within the hollow of my hands.

Abe never again wrote poetry, and he was so dissatisfied with this first collection that he refused ever to allow it to be reprinted. The poems, included in the edition of his complete works that appeared after his death, represent a minor part of his art, but they are among the rare works in which he permitted himself a lyrical, romantic tone. Although the expression in his novels was sometimes poetic, he was fundamentally a writer of prose, much more likely to describe sex than love. He tended to write about things rather than emotions. The beginning of his story "Beyond the Curve" (Kābu no mukō; later incorporated into the novel *The Ruined Map* [*Moetsukita chizu*]) displays this tendency at its most extreme:

Slowly I came to a halt, as if springs in the air were holding me back. My weight, which had started shifting from my left toes to my right heel, came flowing backward again, settling heavily in the region of my left knee. The incline was good and steep.

The road was surfaced not in asphalt but in rough concrete, with narrow grooves at four-inch intervals to prevent cars from skidding. But that did pedestrians little good. Besides, the rough texture of the concrete was effectively smoothed out by deposits of dust and tire scraps. On a rainy day, in old, rubber-soled shoes, the going would be slippery. Still, these grooves could make a significant difference if you were driving. They could be just what was needed in winter, draining off excess water from melting snow and ice.*

---

*Kōbō Abe, *Beyond the Curve*, trans. Juliet Winters Carpenter (New York: Kodansha International, 1991), p. 223.

The description is objective, rather in the mood of the *nouveau roman* of Robbe-Grillet, but Abe was by no means an impassive witness. His essays make clear his profound concern with developments in the world, but he chose not to express this concern on the surface of his novels. The difficulties that many people experience in reading his novels and plays do not stem from the language he used, which is generally perfectly clear, but from the unspoken meanings, which Abe hoped the reader would sense even when the writing seemed absolutely bare.

In the years following the war, it was by no means clear if Abe would ever be able to earn a living by writing works of literary intent. He was obliged to turn out a stream of children's stories, radio dramas, anything at all that would bring in money. These early works, like the poems, were unknown until a few years ago, when the diligent editor of the *Complete Works* uncovered them. In later years, after Abe had established his reputation as a novelist, he totally refused to write occasional pieces, perhaps recalling his years in the galleys.

The poverty in which he lived probably made Abe more susceptible to joining the Communist Party. It was also the one political party that preached internationalism. It is not clear exactly when he joined. Although thanks to the American Occupation, any Japanese could join the Communist Party freely, not all employers welcomed persons who were known to be party members, and a clandestine atmosphere surrounded membership in the party. Abe probably did not worry too much when he joined the party that his writings might be affected by membership in an organization that was known for its insistence on party discipline. It is inconceivable to me that he would ever have accepted directives as to what he might write. This was the period when the leaders of the Japanese Communist Party were doing their best to make their party seem "lovable," and they do not seem to have attempted to coerce writers into mouthing party doctrines.

Abe's works of the immediate postwar period are at times openly left-wing, but the political message is certainly less striking than the avant-garde techniques he employed. Most of the writers and other intellectuals of his generation, probably as a result of the war, were affected by Marxism. The leftward shift of literature after the war was not, of course, unique to Japan. Postwar Japanese authors, again in contact with world literature after the war years, turned to the French first of all and discovered that many important writers, headed by Sartre, were sympathetic to Marxism. Those Japanese who were attracted instead to American literature were likely to turn to John Dos Passos, Sinclair Lewis, or Upton Sinclair, all of whom, at least during one period of their careers, had openly expressed left-wing convictions. To Japanese who had suffered through years of right-wing fanaticism, the left wing seemed humane by comparison, and anything was better than a revival of militarism.

The writings of many Japanese authors who would later be associated with quite different political views, or with no political views whatsoever, were often colored during the postwar era by a specifically proletarian ideology. What was more natural than for an author describing the burned-out slums of Tokyo to express bitterness over the wartime ideology that had caused such misery or to express the hope that a new and democratic Japan, hand in hand with other progressive nations, would bring equality to all?

A typical feature of literature of the postwar era was the formation of groups of like-minded authors. Usually the common bond among the authors was political rather than specifically literary, and some writers who are now totally forgotten exercised power because of their political stance. The groups to which Abe belonged, however, consisted mainly of writers and critics of distinction, not party hacks. In 1951 Abe published several of his best-known stories, including "The Wall; The Crime of S. Karma" (Kabe; S. Karuma shi no hanzai) and "The Red Cocoon" (Akai mayu), each of which won a literary prize, including the most important for a young writer, the Akutagawa Prize, often the first step in a successful career.

In the same year, Abe wrote the short story "The Intruders" (Chinnyū-sha). It is the story of a family that invades the apartment of a young man—professing to do this for his sake—takes over his life, and eventually kills him. The work was obviously allegorical, and readers probably had no difficulty identifying the intruders as Americans and the victim the people of one or another country where America had intervened. This was Abe's first work to be translated (into Czech). Sixteen years later, in 1967, Abe developed this short story into the full-length play entitled *Friends* (*Tomodachi*). By this time, his political outlook had changed considerably (he was expelled from the Communist Party in 1961, the year that *The Woman in the Dunes* was published). The intruding family were now recognizable as Communists, not as Americans. Although translations of the play were made into several languages of the Soviet bloc, they could not be published or performed until much later.

Abe's political views began to shift in 1956 when he was invited to Czechoslovakia to attend a writers' conference. Abe profoundly admired the writings of Franz Kafka, and when he learned that the Czech minister of education was a specialist in Kafka, he contrasted him with the undistinguished men who had held the equivalent position in Japan. He felt new admiration for a system under which such an appointment could be made. However, the Soviet Union's suppression of the Hungarian revolt in 1956 against Communist rule could not be ignored by a man of his honesty, and for the first time he began to consider the contradictions between Communism as a philosophy and Communism as a form of government.

Another important factor in his change of belief was the result of his meeting in Moscow with his Russian translator. As a guest of the state, Abe had a room in the best hotel, and (unlike ordinary tourists and other visitors of the time) he did not have to wait two hours in the hotel dining room for his meal to be served. Everywhere he went in the Soviet Union, he was met with deference and friendliness as a distinguished visitor. Most Japanese writers who received this treatment were too pleased and grateful ever to probe beneath the surface, but gradually, bit by bit, Abe learned from his translator what life in the Soviet Union was really like — the knock on the door at two in the morning, the years of imprisonment without cause or trial, the constant fear. These revelations shook Abe, but he had no choice but to admit the truth of what he had been told.

Some years later, when I myself visited the Soviet Union for the first time, Abe gave me the translator's name and address. I was unsuccessful in my attempts to reach her by telephone but found my way to her apartment. I rang the bell. There was no response. I rang again, but there was still no response. I tore a page from my notebook and started to write a message in Japanese, our common language, telling her where I was staying, when suddenly the door opened. The translator's husband, observing me through a peephole, realized when he saw me writing Japanese that I was not from the police. I became friendly with the Russian translator, from whom I also learned much about the Soviet Union, and when I published my own translation of Abe's play *Friends*, I dedicated it to her, using only her initials lest she be harmed.

In 1957 Abe published a book on his travels in Eastern Europe, the first of his works to deal squarely with the contradiction between the professed aims of a socialist society and the forms of those aims when put into practice. He eventually concluded that the ideals of socialism were corrupted when they became instruments of the state. He still considered himself to be radical and, in his essays, warned repeatedly of the danger of a revival of what he called the right-wing inquisition; but he was no longer bound by any ideology. In 1967 he joined with Mishima Yukio (a conservative), Kawabata Yasunari (a liberal), and Ishikawa Jun (a conservative radical) in signing a protest against the Great Cultural Revolution in China.

This political activity did not interfere with Abe's literary production, and he won coveted literary prizes for not only his novels but also his plays. His first play to be staged was *The Uniform* (*Seifuku*, 1955). Abe told me in an interview how he had come to write this play. In response to my question of what led him to write this first play, he replied:

It was an accident. I had no intention whatsoever of writing a play, but I had no choice. It happened rather early in my career as a writer. I was asked by a magazine for a short story, but somehow I couldn't manage to write anything. As the deadline approached, I became more and more frantic. At the time I still had trouble selling my stories, and

I was worried that if I failed to meet the deadline, I would never again be asked for another. The night before the deadline I was absolutely desperate, when suddenly it occurred to me that it might be easier to work out something if all I had to do was to write dialogue, and I didn't have to trouble myself with descriptions and the rest. I threw away everything I had written up to then, and in a great hurry composed a piece consisting entirely of dialogue. It took about three hours. This was my first play, called *The Uniform*. I had no previous experience as a dramatist, and Japanese magazine editors have an extreme aversion to publishing plays, especially by unknown writers. If I had told them in advance that I planned to write a play, they probably would have refused to print it. But with the deadline at hand, the magazine could not very well refuse to accept my manuscript. So, much against the editor's wishes, they published it. Purely by accident, the play came to the attention of a producer who asked to stage it. The production was rather well received, and I later had requests for plays from various theatrical groups.

Abe had had no training as a playwright and probably had seen very few plays performed before he wrote one, but he instinctively knew what would be effective on the stage (or in a radio drama). At first his plays were directed by professionals, but in 1973 he founded the Abe Studio for training actors and actresses in the techniques of performance he had evolved and for staging the plays he wrote during the next six or seven years. His "method" proved to be so successful that several established actors joined the company in order to benefit from his guidance. Abe considered the plays to be an important part of his work. He told me during our interview:

> As far as I am concerned, my plays are as necessary and as important as my novels. But I don't think of my work in the theater as being confined to writing the plays. Most playwrights have traditionally felt that their responsibility ended when they delivered a finished play to

the producer, but I do not distinguish all that much between a play and the performance. In my case it is not so much a contrast between writings plays and novels as between working in the theater and writing novels. Both have the same importance. If either was missing from my life, it would bother me.

Abe spent day after day at the studio, often from morning to night, guiding the actors in intonation, movement, interpretation. The studio was open at all times, and the actors could therefore drop in whenever it was convenient to practice calisthenics, declamation, or any other aspect of performance. Abe emphasized movement, as opposed to the more naturalistic theater, and after 1976 he displayed an increasing interest in nonliterary plays. *The Little Elephant Is Dead* (*Kozō wa shinda*, 1979) pushed this concept to its furthest development: it is plotless and virtually without dialogue, depending instead on the movements of the actors, the lighting, and the music to arouse responses in the audience. Abe believed that this was the particular function of the theater. In 1979 his company performed the work in Japan and in four American cities. It relied so little on dialogue that there was virtually no language barrier, and the response of American audiences was overwhelmingly favorable. Abe told me—but again I felt impelled to take his statements with a grain of salt—that there were fistfights at the box office over who would get tickets. After the company had returned to Japan and was performing in Tokyo, Abe wrote a brief statement concerning his objectives. It opened, "This work represents the end results achieved during the seven years since I first began to participate in all aspects of theatrical activity. At the same time, it is a point of departure." He expressed the conviction that literature had usurped the original purpose of theater and that critics who insisted that a play must have a "meaning" that they could analyze were anachronisms in a world in which "meaning" was not required of works of literature. Although he stated that *The Little Elephant Is Dead* was the beginning for future explorations in nonliterary theater, it was in fact his last play. He returned to being a novelist, a man of words rather than a man of the theater. Perhaps he found that he had actually reached the limits of what could be achieved without dialogue or a plot; the work seemed likely to turn into modern dance rather than into plays. He had been successful in these late plays (and a film based on one of them), but at a cost of sacrificing his most precious asset, his marvelous skill with words.

During the remaining fourteen years of his life—from 1979 to 1993—Abe devoted himself to fiction and the occasional essay. Increasingly, he had become to editors a maddeningly slow writer by Japanese standards; he kept rewriting his manuscripts again and again until he was at last ready to allow them leave his hands. From the early 1980s, he was helped by the use of a word processor—the first Japanese author to use this convenience—which made it possible for him to correct a page of manuscript without having to rewrite the whole page from the beginning, as had been his perfectionist custom; but the ease of corrections may in the end have induced him to tinker with the expression even more than before. He completed only two novels during these fourteen years, *The Ark* Sakura (*Hakobune* Sakura *maru*) and *Kangaroo Notebook* (*Kangarū nōto*). Neither of these novels was successful with the general public, but *Kangaroo Notebook*, in my opinion, is one of his major achievements.

Abe's novels have never been great favorites with people who seek from fiction nothing more than entertainment or with commuters hoping to make the two-hour journey to work pass more quickly, but he has had a solid following and could count on sales of at least 100,000 copies for his novels. It is amazing that avant-garde works should have sold so well. But as they became more difficult, many readers who bought them because of the prestige of Abe's name did not always read them to the end, and the critics often regretted that he had abandoned the easily followed narrative style of *The Woman in the Dunes* or *The Face of Another* for new experiments. But Abe was determined that his novels not be viewed merely as Japanese examples of some world trend in literature. Instead, he wanted to *make* the trends, even if this meant that his books would not be fully appreciated until some future time. When I casually mentioned to an editor that I had enjoyed *Kangaroo Notebook*, the story of a man with a strange malady—radish sprouts coming from his shins—he begged me to write an article for *Shinchō*, the literary monthly published by the company, because no one else had praised it. Probably my friendship with Abe had enabled me to understand, better than most critics, that this novel, so full of humor, is about death, and specifically about Abe's own death.

Abe had always seemed unusually robust and youthful for his age. Although he spent countless hours poring over his manuscripts, he never gave the impression of an author who worked in a cork-lined study. He loved his cars and enjoyed driving, especially under difficult conditions. In 1986 at the Tenth International Inventors' Exhibition in New York, in competition with inventors of everything from airplane engines to laser microscopes, he was awarded a silver medal for a device he had invented for changing tires.

Abe was an extremely skillful photographer, as exhibitions at Columbia University and in Tokyo demonstrated. He was uninterested in the usual subjects—the beauties of nature or the faces of people. His pictures most often show the end of a process, the lonely remains that reveal what has been. When in 1978 he arrived in Milwaukee in order to attend the performances of his play *Friends*, he was asked what he would like to see in the city. He answered, "The garbage dump." People took this for a joke, or perhaps as a sly comment on Milwaukee, but I believe that he meant it quite literally. More than picturesque sites along Lake Michigan or the art museum, the dump would have told him about life in Milwaukee. Among his photographs of Japan, I am particularly moved by one series showing the debris of an abandoned coal mine, and another showing members of a family somberly pushing a wheelchair through the bright grounds of the Osaka Exposition.

In his last years, Abe was constantly battling against illness. He told me, as a great secret, that he had cancer. He hated letting people know he was unwell, and he probably was afraid of death. His classmates at medical school, now distinguished physicians, did everything possible to save his life, but (perhaps because of the treatment) he aged very markedly and tottered rather than walked. It was painful to see this. But once seated in a coffee shop, he was still fun to be with. His sense of humor, especially his wonderful irony, set him apart from any other Japanese writer I have known. He never agreed with anything I said, however innocuous. If I commented that it was hot, he was likely to prove statistically that it was unusually cool for that time of year; if I said that prices were high, he would demonstrate that they had been falling constantly. Despite his illness, Abe was as alert and funny as always, and he seems to have continued writing until shortly before his death. Several incomplete manuscripts were found in his word processor, all of them interesting and unique to Abe.

Abe and I enjoyed each other's company. Sometimes, when he discovered my abysmal ignorance of even the rudimentary facts of science, he would shake his head in amazement, declaring that every Japanese middle-school student was familiar with what, for me, was unknown territory. But he seemed to value my opinions on his books. At his request I wrote blurbs for some of his novels and later wrote the *kaisetsu*, or "expository comments," appended to almost all his novels and plays when they went into paper. We also did together a series of dialogues that were gathered into a book. When I look at these documents of our friendship, I feel proud my name is joined to his. Proud but very sad, for I lost in Abe a strange and wonderful friend.

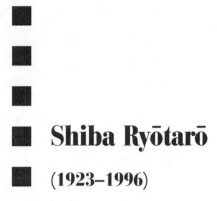

Shiba Ryōtarō

(1923–1996)

I don't really remember when I first met Shiba Ryōtarō. Quite possibly it was between 1953 and 1955 while I was studying at Kyoto University and Shiba was working as a reporter at the Kyoto office of the *Sankei shimbun*. Foreign students were something of a rarity in Kyoto, and it would not have been strange if Shiba, like other reporters I remember more clearly, had interviewed me, if only to ask my impressions of Japan.

In those days I was frequently asked, by virtually every reporter in the city, whatever had made me learn Japanese and if I did not find life in Kyoto extremely inconvenient. Reporters were always eager to elicit from foreigners unfavorable comments about Japan, but perhaps by way of compensation, they were equally eager to take photographs of foreigners struggling with chopsticks.

Even if Shiba subjected me to the treatment appropriate to a typical foreigner—which I doubt—I have, in all honesty, no recollection of him from those days. I think I would have remembered him if only for the shock of white hair that even at that time was his most conspicuous visible feature.

My first real memory of Shiba dates from the time of our "dialogue" in 1971. An editor at Chūō Kōron Sha with whom I was friendly telephoned one day to report that he had a marvelous idea but pledged me to secrecy. The insistence on secrecy made me more than usually attentive to his proposal, but when he revealed its contents—a dialogue between Shiba

and myself, dialogues being a frequent feature of Japanese publications —
I was nonplussed. I had to admit that not only had I never read a word by
Shiba but I knew nothing about even the kind of books he wrote. I politely
declined to take part in the dialogue.

The editor was disappointed, but two or three days later he again telephoned to report that Shiba, though an extremely busy man, not only was
willing to have a dialogue with me but, when told that I was unfamiliar
with his writings, had insisted that I was not to read them. This gracious
concession made it impossible for me not to take part in the dialogue.
Shiba imposed only one condition, that he not be obliged to move out of
the Kansai region during the anticipated three sessions of our dialogue. I
gladly complied.

We met first among the recently excavated ruins of Heijō, the ancient
capital, not far from Nara. Our guide informed us of such matters as the
likelihood that two rows of stones in a field were the foundations of the
Hall of State and the likelihood that another cluster of stones was the site
of a temple. I knew in advance that I would not retain this information for
more than twenty minutes, but I listened patiently, from time to time steal-
ing glances at Shiba. I thought that his white hair, contrasting with his
youthful face, gave him a pleasing dignity. When we spoke, his tone was
friendly and (unlike many others who met me for the first time), he did
not seem to worry over whether or not I would understand his Japanese.

After inspecting the ruins of the Heijō capital, we went into the city of
Nara where our dialogue was to take place. There we exchanged views
over dinner for a couple of hours, every word being taken down by both a
stenographer and a tape recorder. When the dialogue was over and I went
to my room at a nearby inn, I felt quite discouraged, sure that my part in
the dialogue had been a total failure. In fact, I could not recall having said
one word to Shiba apart from an occasional "Of course" or "Is that so?" I
had been overwhelmed by the mass of information at Shiba's command
with which he inundated me with his every utterance. Even as I was trying
to think of something to say in response to one of his revelations, another

great wave of information would come sweeping down over me. I was no match for him.

Only later, when I examined the transcript of our dialogue, did I realize that although I had been so tense at the time that I could not recall anything I had said, in fact I had spoken quite a lot. Moreover, I now realized that Shiba had again and again thoughtfully provided me with opportunities to display whatever knowledge I might possess. I had been too intimidated by his range of knowledge to recognize this kindness, the first of many instances I was to experience.

In the preface he wrote to the book *The Japanese and Japanese Culture* (*Nihonjin to nihon bunka*), which came out of the three dialogues, Shiba said that our only mutually shared experience up to the time we met was our both having served during the war—we had been "comrades in arms" (*sen'yū*). It was certainly unusual to say we had been "comrades in arms." After all, we were on opposing sides and had never so much as seen each other. But Shiba was right. We had shared the experience of a terrible war, and the experience had changed us equally. In my case, as Shiba mentioned, it was because of the war that I had learned Japanese, and this would be at once my lifework and the factor that made it possible for Shiba and me to become friends. In his case (though he did not mention it at this time) the war had aroused a hatred for the nationalism that had been its cause. Our wartime experiences had been entirely different, but they had brought us to the same place.

I think I felt drawn to Shiba—even though the first two of the three dialogues were certainly a strain—because he reminded me somehow of my teacher, Tsunoda Ryūsaku *sensei*. The two men did not look in the least alike, and they belonged to entirely different generations. For that matter, their interest in Japanese history and religion was by no means the same; but both men constantly searched for what was truly important, truly worth remembering in the events of history. Both men also relied on intuition when they found that the bare facts were insufficient to permit understanding. Intuition is a dangerous guide, but there are times when it is worth the risk of following it. A work dependent on intuition may be seriously flawed, but it is likely to be more interesting and perhaps more truthful than a mere accumulation of facts.

The first dialogue between Shiba and me began with an editor giving us a general plan, but we followed no particular order in the matters we discussed, one subject leading to another. I soon discovered from his comments and questions that although Shiba had forbidden me to read his books, he had taken the trouble to read several of mine and therefore knew which topics were most likely to interest me. The book based on the three dialogues (the first held in Nara, the second in Kyoto, and the third in Osaka) was published in May 1972. It opens in this manner:

Shiba: Today the two of us came to Nara and looked over the remains of the Heijō capital together. I felt as I looked at the ruins how amazing it was that Japan, which at that time produced hardly anything apart from rice in the paddies—a country that was economically so poor it was little more than fields and forests—was able to build a capital of that size. But I suppose that the purpose of the capital was rather similar to that of what today might be called a world's fair.*

Keene: Yes, it probably was something like that. The first big temple in Japan was the Shitennō-ji. It was built to receive foreign visitors, to demonstrate to people from advanced countries—especially Chinese— that Japan had a culture, that it was capable of building such a splendid temple. I imagine the same was true of the Heijō capital. The Japanese probably feared that if they didn't build such a capital, they would be thought of as barbarians who lived in a backward country. It was probably for the same reason—a strong desire to prove to the outside world

---

*Shiba's mention of a "world's fair" (*bankokuhaku*) was probably inspired by the extremely successful Osaka Exposition of the year before.

that Japan had a history and a literature—that the *Nihon shoki*, the *Man'yōshū*, and the *Kaifūsō*, the imperial collection of poems in Chinese, were compiled.*

As I read over these and later exchanges, I can see now that Shiba had made it possible for me to discuss something of special interest to me, Japanese concern about how their country was viewed by people in the outside world, the kind of topic a non-Japanese like myself is likely to find absorbing. Shiba must also have been thinking of the many Japanese attempts over the centuries to gain the respect of advanced countries. This was true not only in the seventh century, when the Heijō capital was built, but also in the nineteenth century after the Meiji Restoration and was equally true of Japan at the time we had our dialogue.

My words, as recorded by the stenographer, were surprising even to myself. I can't recall that I had previously thought that the compilation of three famous eighth-century works had been inspired by the desire to prove that Japan was a civilized country. Perhaps I had heard this long ago from Tsunoda *sensei*, or it may have been an unprepared response to the stimulus of Shiba's comments. Japanese editors who arrange dialogues between strangers always hope that one participant's remarks will stimulate the other to express thoughts that otherwise would lie dormant within him. On reading the dialogue now, thirty years later, I am surprised at my boldness and glad that Shiba had provided me with the occasion for making such an observation.

About twenty years after this first meeting with Shiba, the same publisher arranged for a three-way conversation (*teidan*) in connection with the forthcoming publication of a series of books devoted to Japan during the Tokugawa period. In addition to Shiba and me, the critic and play-

---

*Shiba Ryōtarō and Donarudo Kīn, *Nihonjin to nihon bunka* (Tokyo: Chūō Kōron Sha, 1967), p. 4.

wright Yamazaki Masakazu took part. The site was Ichiriki, the famous teahouse in Gion where Ōishi Kuranosuke is said to have amused himself while plotting vengeance against his enemy, the man who insulted his lord. I was excited to be in this celebrated restaurant, to which guests are normally admitted only if they possess the proper introductions, but I was dismayed when the *teidan* was about to start to hear Shiba say, "I don't like the Tokugawa period." Yamazaki said, "I don't like it either." Since the point of the *teidan* was to create interest in the Tokugawa period among potential purchasers of the series, it was not an auspicious beginning to our conversation. I was left to defend the period in terms of the writers I admired and had made my specialty—Chikamatsu and Bashō especially. But the *teidan* got nowhere, and even the capable editor had trouble in finding enough substance for an article in his magazine.

Afterward I wondered why Shiba had spoken so harshly about the Tokugawa period. It occurred to me that although he had written extensively about the period just before the establishment of the Tokugawa shogunate and also about the period when the shogunate was tottering and on the verge of collapse, he had not written about the more than two hundred years of Tokugawa peace. Perhaps this was because peace is less exciting to a novelist than warfare and change, but I think it was mainly because he disliked the constricted life that the Tokugawa government imposed on the Japanese people in order to preserve the stability of the regime. Some of the great writers and artists of that time, unable to fit into Tokugawa society, lived on the periphery as recluses or eccentrics or as frequenters of the world of the licensed quarters. At our distance from Tokugawa society, we can forget its repressive nature and enjoy the haiku of Bashō, the plays of Chikamatsu, or the prints of Utamaro and Sharaku without concerning ourselves with the conditions under which these works were created. For Shiba, though, the chief characteristic of the Tokugawa period was not its art or literature but its lack of freedom and its isolation from the rest of the world; it was a time marked by the oppression of the human spirit.

Shiba's likes and dislikes were sometimes revealed indirectly. A whole series of books is devoted to his travels within Japan, and another series describes his travels abroad. Wherever he went, he always found things to admire, and often the choice of things he admired in foreign countries indirectly revealed a criticism of Japan. I recall especially his account of his travels in the Basque region of France and Spain. There was a reason for a Japanese to be particularly interested in the Basques. St. Francis Xavier, the most celebrated of the Spanish and Portuguese missionaries to visit Japan in the sixteenth century, was a Basque, and Shiba mentioned another Basque who had contributed to Japanese culture, the missionary Sauveur Candau, who acquired a remarkable facility in the Japanese language and was admired by Shiba, who considered Father Candau to be a benefactor of Japan.*

It is surprising, all the same, that Shiba devoted so much attention to the Basques, a people who were seldom discussed by the Japanese except in terms of the curious theory that because the Basque and Japanese languages are not related to any other languages, they must be mutually related.

Shiba's interest in the Basques was aroused by the fact that they had a language and an ancient culture, but no country of their own. As we know from the tragic events of recent years, the Basques have by no means been satisfied to be without a country, but Shiba was attracted by the possibility that the identity and culture of a people could survive without the nationalism that was the curse of the modern world. Of course, he was aware that Basque extremists had resorted to acts of terror in the hopes of gaining complete independence, but he seems to have hoped that somehow the Basques and their culture could survive without demanding the political independence that inevitably develops into nationalism. This hope exemplified his humanitarianism and his deep dislike for the divisiveness of

---

*Sauveur Antoine Candau (1897–1955) arrived in Japan in 1925 and, except for the war years, was in Japan from then until his death. He wrote books in Japanese (Shiba praised his style) and compiled a Latin–Japanese lexicon.

nationalism that pits country against country, culture against culture. Abe Kōbō, who almost never praised another writer, was impressed by the attitude underlying Shiba's description of the Basques, no doubt because he also thought of nationalism as the greatest obstacle to peace in the world.

Perhaps it was his acquaintance with Candau that had first aroused Shiba's interest in the Basques. He expressed his admiration for Candau in these terms:

> S. Candau was a priest and a theologian, and he was also a philosopher, but even more, he was a splendid "Japanese." From the time he landed in Japan in 1925, he enjoyed the great affection and respect even of nonbelievers, and he in turn loved the Japanese and Japanese culture. In addition, he wrote a perfect Japanese prose style that had a high order of content and a fine quality of humor. On top of that, he was the possessor of a gentle and transparent soul.*

I do not think Shiba was being humorous when he spoke of Candau as a Japanese. Rather, I think he believed that a foreigner who spoke Japanese perfectly and who loved Japanese culture should be accepted as a Japanese, regardless of his facial features. I believe that he also hoped that this possibility should not be limited to Candau but extended to every non-Japanese who wished to be accepted as a Japanese and that the more such "new Japanese" there were, the more likely it would be that the mystique of the single, homogeneous Japanese race would cease to spread nationalistic prejudices.

Shiba was one of the proponents of the Yamagata Bantō Prize offered by Osaka Prefecture. The prize is intended to express Japanese appreciation of the work of foreign scholars who have devoted their lives to the study of

---

*Shiba Ryōtarō, *Kaidō wo yuku* 8:16, in *Shiba Ryōtarō zenshū*, vol. 59 (Tokyo: Bungei Shunjū Sha, 1999).

Japan. In 1982 I was the first to receive the prize. I do not know why I, rather than some other scholar, was chosen for the prize, but I feel sure that Shiba, whose great kindness I had again and again experienced, had something to do with this decision.

In the same year, 1982, Shiba and I participated in a symposium held under the auspices of the *Asahi shimbun*. After the symposium, all the participants went to a restaurant where we were offered dinner and ample saké. I was seated not far from the president. Shiba, who seemed to have been drinking rather more than usual, came up to us from the opposite end of the room and said in a fairly loud voice to the president, "The *Asahi shimbun* is no good!" Everyone looked at him in surprise. He continued, "In the Meiji period, the *Asahi* was no good, but it became a good newspaper by hiring Natsume Sōseki. The only way for the *Asahi* to become a good newspaper today is to hire Donald Keene."

Everybody laughed and attributed these remarks to Shiba's tipsiness, but a week or so later, to my astonishment, I was offered a job with the *Asahi* as a guest editor. I accepted, beginning a happy ten years of association with the *Asahi*. Needless to say, I was extremely grateful to Shiba, but I was puzzled as to what I might contribute to the *Asahi* that would justify his linking me with the great novelist Natsume Sōseki. Gradually I came to realize it was not so much that he believed I would be able to write outstanding articles for the newspaper as that he hoped my presence would give it a more international quality. Although those who worked for the *Asahi* naturally were proud of their newspaper and believed that its concern with international matters was fully attested by its many correspondents who reported on developments abroad, not one non-Japanese was writing for the *Asahi* in Japan.

Shiba once remarked to me that it might do the staff of the *Asahi* good if I ate in the employees' cafeteria, in this way bringing home to the other *Asahi* employees eating there that they had a colleague who, though a foreigner, was as much a part of the organization as a Japanese. I accordingly ate in the cafeteria a couple of times, but I confess that I could not detect any effect resulting from this gesture. Everyone on the *Asahi* was friendly, and I think I contributed to the newspaper with the four serials I wrote during the following years, but my presence was not enough to make the *Asahi* more—or less—international. It was typical of Shiba to have hoped that even one person could affect a large organization. Perhaps if I had had the qualifications to participate in discussions of politics and economics with other members of the *Asahi* staff, I might have better fulfilled Shiba's hope that I would be an agent of internationalism.

In a sense it was strange that Shiba should have been so eager to make Japan more international. His enormous popularity as a novelist and essayist stemmed not from his advocacy of internationalism but from his ability to reassure Japanese, stunned by both defeat in war and the rejection of traditional values, that they could be proud of their history and the great men of Japan. Behind this success was the long Japanese tradition of presenting history in the garb of fiction.

The Japanese fondness for historical fiction goes back at least as far as *A Tale of Flowering Fortunes* (*Eiga monogatari*), written in the eleventh century. This long, rambling work presents not only the bare bones of history—births and deaths, promotions and demotions, and the like—but also the poetry composed on various occasions and, most interestingly, the private conversations of great figures of state, even those held in places where no historian could have overheard them. *The Great Mirror* (*Ōkagami*), written a little later, opens as two exceedingly old men—one 180 years old and the other 170 years old—reminisce about events known to them from long ago. Most of their anecdotes, though of literary interest, cannot be taken seriously as history, if only because the narrators, despite their great age, could not possibly have seen or heard what they describe. In any case, the purpose of the unknown author was essentially literary: few of the memorable events in *The Great Mirror* can be accepted as historical truth.

The *Tale of the Heike*, the closest the Japanese ever came to composing an epic, was an artistic re-creation of the warfare that had occurred at the end of the twelfth century between the Taira and Minamoto clans. In general, it follows a course of historical events that can be verified from other sources, but it also contains innumerable conversations and even unspoken thoughts that could only have been the products of the authors' imagination. The story, declaimed to musical accompaniment (normally by a recitant-priest), grew richer in description and human interest as successive generations of recitants expanded the text, until what may have been originally a bare account of who killed whom became a major work of literature.

Shiba's historical fiction followed a rather similar development. He first amassed a large collection of source materials that he carefully read over until he was thoroughly familiar with the facts behind the story he was about to relate; but once he actually began writing, he did not hesitate when necessary to intuit what the characters in his stories had thought or said on a particular occasion. The resulting works were exciting in a way rarely true of the documents that were his sources, and as a result his books regularly became best-sellers. Japanese readers found in his novels not only the excitement of a good story effectively told but the pleasure of having their past restored to them. This was particularly true of readers at the time when Shiba began writing: the Japanese heritage had been either totally discarded or else reduced to the childish fantasy of costume movies.

The figures from the past whom Shiba resuscitated were not fictitious; they were for the most part unknown to his readers, but he made them and the drama of their times come alive. He helped the Japanese discover that their country's history did not consist solely of the heroics of sworded adversaries. His heroes had intelligence and ideals, and if they used their swords, it was not simply to display their skill at fencing.

It has been annoying to some Japanese, especially those who would name Shiba as their favorite author, that his works are not known abroad. They sometimes attribute this neglect to the foreign preference for exoticism or the desire to think of Japan in terms of the fragile evocations of a Kawabata novel. They wonder why foreigners cannot appreciate the excitement of a Shiba novel, which is much closer to the Japanese of today than a novel by Tanizaki or Kawabata. But even the most enthusiastic Japanese admirers of Shiba's writings never mentioned his name as a possible recipient of a Nobel Prize; and naturally, the Swedish Academy had not heard of a writer whose works, with minor exceptions, had never been translated into English. Although many Japanese, including persons of unquestioned critical discrimination, were convinced that Shiba was a major writer and deplored the foreign ignorance of his works, his works were not included in typical collections of masterpieces of modern Japanese literature and were not discussed by serious Japanese critics. This tended to dampen the interest of foreign scholars in his novels.

The admiration of Shiba by the Japanese public at large has not abated. It often happens in Japan that interest in a writer's works markedly diminishes after his death, but this has not been true of Shiba. Soon after he died in 1996, many bookshops set aside a special corner where his works were displayed. This was not the first time such a corner had been created: they are fairly common immediately after a prominent writer's death or after he has won the Nobel Prize. Usually the corner disappears after a few weeks, when journalistic interest in the author has petered out, but in Shiba's case his corner seems to have become a permanent feature of bookshops. Not content with publishing new editions of his books, publishers have desperately sought to create "new" works by and about Shiba, extracting his philosophy of life from his writings or collecting the heartwarming reminiscences of his friends.

Admiration of Shiba's novels and essays is very much intertwined with admiration for Shiba the man. He is as close to being a twentieth-century hero as the Japanese possess. Unlike more typical heroes, he remained modest, never calling attention to himself or his books, but forever seeking to understand the nature of Japan. His writings brought Japanese readers the satisfaction of discovering their own history, but it was also important to them that it was Shiba who had made the discovery. His novels often contain digressions, labeled as such; but even though they interrupt the narration, they are welcome to readers because they tell the reader something about Shiba himself, or at least about the associations that a particular event aroused in his memory. He is very much a participant in his writings.

For most foreign readers, however, Shiba's personality is not of such great interest, and the digressions may not seem justified. They may even find that his works suffer from not having had the benefit of a good editor. Repetitions are not unusual, but information that readers should possess at the beginning of a novel is sometimes not revealed until late in the work, and then only casually. These faults—if they are faults—may puzzle or irritate non-Japanese, but they do not distress Japanese readers, who are carried along by the movement of Shiba's prose and by their confidence in him as the author.

Japanese who had complained because Shiba's works were unknown in foreign countries were naturally pleased when they learned that a program had been initiated by the Japanese government to sponsor translations. However, when the first translations finally appeared, the reviews were mostly negative. This was not the fault of the translations: Eileen Kato's translations of four novellas published as *Drunk as a Lord* (*Yotte sōrō*) are in particular admirable, in every way worthy of the originals. The main stumbling block to appreciating Shiba's writings abroad seems to be the difference in the expectations of Japanese and non-Japanese readers with respect to the characters who appear in his works of historical fiction. For example, non-Japanese readers are likely to have trouble sympathizing with and feeling respect for a daimyo who, though he is reputed to be distinguished by his intelligence and accomplishments, is portrayed as a chronic drunkard and who, on occasion, unable to hold his liquor, vomits uninhibitedly. Conversely, Japanese readers may consider this a regrettable but harmless flaw in the daimyo's character; they may even feel closer to Yamanouchi Yōdō because of an all-too-human failing. Western readers, however, being unaccustomed to vomiting heroes, may find Yamanouchi Yōdō repulsive. Again, when Shiba scrupulously notes that Tokugawa Yoshinobu, the last shogun, a man he obviously admires, always sent for a prostitute as soon as he was settled in lodgings for the night, Western readers may experience a momentary shock, although for the Japanese of the past this would have been considered perfectly acceptable behavior. It is to Shiba's credit that he did not falsify his portraits of Yōdō and Yoshinobu in the hope of endearing them to readers, nor did he resort to anachronisms in the manner of another Japanese writer of historical fiction who had the twelfth-century tyrant Taira Kiyomori deplore the lack of progress in Japan.

The task of the translator of Shiba's historical fiction is to go beyond understanding the text and to render it in acceptable English. A novel is apt to contain names and institutions that, though familiar to most Japanese, might baffle Western readers. Should an explanation be silently included in the translated text? Or would footnotes be better? Or should it be left to the readers to guess the meaning? And should the repetitions be pruned?

It probably is easier to translate an invented work by Shiba like *Storm Winds in Tartary* (*Dattan shippū roku*, 1987), which is set largely in Manchuria during the seventeenth century, than a work describing Japanese history of the same period. Because the setting was foreign, Shiba could not count on readers' familiarity with the people and events described, and he therefore explained the customs of the Manchus and related in detail how it was possible for them, a people who numbered no more than a few hundred thousand, to conquer the huge and populous Chinese empire. Shiba had studied Mongolian at the Osaka University of Foreign Languages, and his knowledge of the languages of Central Asia gave convincing authenticity to this novel, but the story was essentially invented by Shiba himself.

This work might be more successful in translation than Shiba's novels treating Japanese of the past. But it is unlikely that *Storm Winds in Tartary*, for all its exciting plot, will ever become one of Shiba's favorites with the Japanese public, for it contains none of the revelations of the characteristics of the Japanese people that gave his historical fiction its special appeal.

The part of Shiba's oeuvre that is most difficult for non-Japanese to appreciate is his style. Shiba wrote in a vivid way that won him readers from the outset of his career. The special quality of this style is largely incommunicable in a translation, however accomplished. Of course, style is the part of any work that is most likely to be lost in translation, but one does not expect to find style of this quality in popular works of historical fiction. Unless the translator succeeds in communicating the style that gave an éclat to Shiba's novels, their great popularity must remain a mystery to the non-Japanese.

The main problem in foreign appreciation of Shiba's novels, however, is that although they supplied a need felt by the Japanese, it was not necessarily a need of foreigners. While reading a work by Shiba, a Japanese is likely to feel again and again something like "This is what it means to be a Japanese." There no longer are samurai in Japan, but the ideals of the samurai are intelligible to Japanese, even those of a distinctly nonsamurai background, who can understand, for example, the reasons that led Kawai Tsugunosuke, a samurai of capability and enlightened views described in Shiba's novel *The Pass* (*Tōge*, 1968), to take up arms against the Meiji government, even though he knew that this action could lead only to disaster and death. Of course, with study a non-Japanese can appreciate why the characters in a Shiba novel appeal to Japanese readers, but this is not the same as immediate recognition.

I admire Shiba's writings, but he lives in my memory less as a novelist than as a wonderful human being. My attitude would disappoint him, for he put a great deal of himself into his works, but it is rarer to find a man like Shiba than a successful novelist. He was a good man and not merely in the conventional sense of doing no wrong. His writings inspired a whole country, not with patriotic zeal, but with a quiet awareness of what being a Japanese has meant through history.

Shiba tended to be pessimistic about the future of Japan, but he gave solace and courage to Japanese, persuading them that the life of even the most ordinary member of society may be worth celebrating. Although Masaoka Chūzaburō, the poignant hero of *The Sound of Peoples' Footsteps* (*Hitobito no ashioto*, 1981), was the adopted son of the great poet Masaoka Shiki, he was devoid of poetic talent and led a most prosaic life. But Shiba, who normally chose for his characters men who had played an active role during a time of historical change, wrote a memorable novel (in two volumes) about a man who otherwise was unknown to history.

Shiba was interested in people wherever he went, as he demonstrated in the series of books describing his travels in many parts of the world, but

Japan was never far from his mind. I think that Shiba, paraphrasing Terence, might have said of himself, "I am a Japanese, and nothing that concerns a Japanese do I deem a matter of indifference to me." This stance helped give his books their extraordinary popularity with Japanese readers; it may also account for the difficulty that some non-Japanese readers have experienced in accounting for his high reputation.

This situation may change with the publication of more translations. It was a privilege to have known such a hero, and I hope that many others, and not only his countrymen, will discover him through his books.

It is hard to know how future critics and readers will evaluate the writings of the five writers I have discussed here. But it is hard for me to resist predicting that they, whose writings are so different, will continue to be remembered and read not only in Japan but in the entire world.

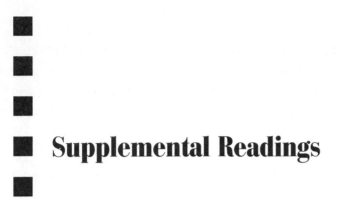

Supplemental Readings

The following titles are recommended to readers who desire a closer acquaintance with the five authors discussed in this book. (Some books, it will be apparent, treat more than one of these authors.) The list is by no means exhaustive.

General

Keene, Donald. *Dawn to the West.* 2nd ed. New York: Columbia University Press, 1998.

Nagashima, Yoichi, ed. *Return to Japan.* Aarhus, Denmark: Aarhus University Press, 2001.

Tsuruta, Kinya, and Thomas E. Swann. *Approaches to the Modern Japanese Novel.* Tokyo: Sophia University, 1976.

Ueda, Makoto. *Modern Japanese Writers.* Stanford, Calif.: Stanford University Press, 1976.

Tanizaki Jun'ichirō

There is, fortunately, a complete bibliography: *Tanizaki in Western Languages: A Bibliography of Translations and Studies,* compiled by Adriana

Boscaro (Ann Arbor: Center for Japanese Studies, University of Michigan, 2000). It lists not only translations but also critical studies of Tanizaki. Many of Tanizaki's works have been translated into English, French, Italian, and other European languages. Among the most important available in English are the following:

A Cat, a Man, and Two Women. Translated by Paul McCarthy. Tokyo: Kodansha International, 1990.

Childhood Years. Translated by Paul McCarthy. Tokyo: Kodansha International, 1988.

Diary of a Mad Old Man. Translated by Howard S. Hibbett. New York: Knopf, 1965.

The Key. Translated by Howard S. Hibbett. New York: Knopf, 1961.

The Makioka Sisters. Translated by Edward G. Seidensticker. New York: Knopf, 1957.

Naomi. Translated by Anthony H. Chambers. New York: Knopf, 1985.

The Reed Cutter and *Captain Shigemoto's Mother*. Translated by Anthony H. Chambers. New York: Knopf, 1994.

The Secret History of the Lord of Musashi and *Arrowroot*. Translated by Anthony H. Chambers. New York: Knopf, 1982.

Seven Japanese Tales. Translated by Howard S. Hibbett. New York: Knopf, 1963.

Some Prefer Nettles. Translated by Edward G. Seidensticker. New York: Knopf, 1955.

Critical Works in English

Boscaro, Adriana, and Anthony H. Chambers, eds. *A Tanizaki Feast: The International Symposium in Venice*. Michigan Monograph Series in Japanese Studies, no. 24. Ann Arbor: Center for Japanese Studies, University of Michigan, 1998.

Chambers, Anthony H. *The Secret Window: Ideals in Tanizaki's Fiction*. Cambridge, Mass.: Harvard University Press, 1994.

Gessel, Van C. *Three Modern Novelists: Sōseki, Tanizaki, Kawabata*. Tokyo: Kodansha International, 1993.

Ito, Ken K. *Visions of Desire: Tanizaki's Fictional Worlds*. Stanford, Calif.: Stanford University Press, 1991.

Kawabata Yasunari

The Dancing Girl of Izu and Other Stories. Translated by J. Martin Holman. Washington, D.C.: Counterpoint, 1977.

The Existence and Discovery of Beauty. Translated by V. H. Viglielmo. Tokyo: *Mainichi* Newspapers, 1969.

House of the Sleeping Beauties and Other Stories. Translated by Edward G. Seidensticker. Tokyo: Kodansha International, 1969.

Japan, the Beautiful, and Myself. Translated by Edward G. Seidensticker. Tokyo: Kodansha International, 1969.

The Master of Go. Translated by Edward G. Seidensticker. New York: Knopf, 1977.

Snow Country. Translated by Edward G. Seidensticker. New York: Knopf, 1956.

The Sound of the Mountain. Translated by Edward G. Seidensticker. New York: Knopf, 1970.

Thousand Cranes. Translated by Edward G. Seidensticker. New York: Knopf, 1970.

Critical Works in English

Petersen, Gwenn Boardman. *The Moon in the Water: Understanding Tanizaki, Kawabata, and Mishima*. Honolulu: University of Hawaii Press, 1979

Mishima Yukio

Acts of Worship: Seven Stories. Translated by John Bester. Tokyo: Kodansha International, 1989.

After the Banquet. Translated by Donald Keene. New York: Knopf, 1963.

Confessions of a Mask. Translated by Meredith Weatherby. New York: New Directions, 1958.

The Decay of the Angel. Translated by Edward G. Seidensticker. New York: Knopf, 1974.

Five Modern Nō Plays. Translated by Donald Keene. New York: Knopf, 1957.

Forbidden Colors. Translated by Alfred H. Marks. New York: Knopf, 1968.

Madame de Sade. Translated by Donald Keene. New York: Grove Press, 1967.

Runaway Horses. Translated by Michael Gallagher. New York: Knopf, 1973.

The Sailor Who Fell from Grace with the Sea. Translated by John Nathan. New York: Knopf, 1965.

Spring Snow. Translated by Michael Gallagher. New York: Knopf, 1972.

Sun and Steel. Translated by John Bester. Tokyo: Kodansha International, 1970.

The Temple of Dawn. Translated by E. Dale Saunders and Cecilia Segawa Seigle. New York: Knopf, 1973.

The Temple of the Golden Pavilion. Translated by Ivan Morris. New York: Knopf, 1959.

Thirst for Love. Translated by Alfred H. Marks. New York: Knopf, 1969.

Critical Works in English

Napier, Susan Jolliffe. *Escape from the Wasteland: Romanticism and Realism in the Fiction of Mishima Yukio and Ōe Kenzaburō.* Cambridge, Mass.: Harvard University Press, 1991.

Nathan, John. *Mishima: A Biography.* Boston: Little, Brown, 1974.

Scott-Stokes, Henry. *The Life and Death of Yukio Mishima.* Rev. ed. New York: Noonday Press, 1995.

Thunman, Noriko. *Forbidden Colors: Essays on Body and Mind in the Novels of Mishima Yukio.* Goteborg: Acta Universitatis Gothoburgensis, 1999.

Yourcenar, Marguerite. *Mishima: A Vision of the Void.* Translated by Alberto Manguel. New York: Farrar, Straus & Giroux, 1986.

Abe Kōbō

The Ark Sakura. Translated by Juliet Winters Carpenter. New York: Knopf, 1988.

Beyond the Curve. Translated by Juliet Winters Carpenter. Tokyo: Kodansha International, 1991.

The Box Man. Translated by E. Dale Saunders. New York: Knopf, 1974.

The Face of Another. Translated by E. Dale Saunders. New York: Knopf, 1966.

Friends. Translated by Donald Keene. New York: Grove Press, 1969.

Kangaroo Notebook. Translated by Maryellen Toman. New York: Knopf, 1996.

The Man Who Turned into a Stick. Translated by Donald Keene. Tokyo: University of Tokyo Press, 1975.

The Ruined Map. Translated by E. Dale Saunders. New York: Knopf, 1969.

Secret Rendezvous. Translated by Juliet Winters Carpenter. New York: Knopf, 1979.

Three Plays. Translated by Donald Keene. New York: Columbia University Press, 1993.

The Woman in the Dunes. Translated by E. Dale Saunders. New York: Knopf, 1964.

Critical Works in English

Iles, Timothy. *Abe Kobo*. Florence: European Press, 2000.

Shields, Nancy K. *Fake Fish: The Theatre of Kobo Abe*. New York: Weatherhill, 1996.

Shiba Ryōtarō

Drunk as a Lord. Translated by Eileen Kato. Tokyo: Kodansha International, 2001.

The Heart Remembers Home. Translated by Eileen Kato. Tokyo: Japan Echo, 1979.

The Last Shogun. Translated by Juliet Winters Carpenter. Tokyo: Kodansha International, 1998.

Index

Kawai Tsugunosuke, 98–99

Keene, Donald: and Abe, 65, 66, 79, 84; *Asahi shimbun*, guest editor for, 93–94; Japanese literature, knowledge of, 1; Mishima's name, method of writing, 48; as recipient of Yamagata Bantō Prize, 92–93; and Shiba, 85–90, 99; and Tanizaki, 2, 3; World War II, effect on, 87

Key, The (*Kagi*,Tanizaki), 20

Kinkaku (Golden Pavilion), 58–61

Kinkakuji (*The Temple of the Golden Pavilion*, Mishima), 24–25, 52, 58–63

kōan (Zen riddles), 59, 62–63

Koga Harue, 37

Komako (fictional character), 38

Lake, The (*Mizuumi*, Kawabata), 27

"Letters to My Parents" (Fubo e no tegami, Kawabata), 35

Literary Discussion Group (Bungei kondan kai), 34–35

literature, 77, 82. *See also* Japanese literature

Little Elephant Is Dead, The (*Kozō wa shinda*, Abe), 81–82

love-death, 53

"Lyric Poem" (Jojōka, Kawabata), 35–37

Madame de Sade (*Sado kōshaku fujin*, Mishima), 57

Makioka Sisters, The (*Sasameyuki*, Tanizaki), 2, 3, 18–19

Manchuria, 67, 73

Masamune Hakuchō, viii

Masaoka Chūzaburō, 99–100

masks, 48–49

masochism, 8

Master of Go, The (*Meijin*, Kawabata), 40

meaning, literature and, 81

Medal of Culture, 19

Meiji Restoration, 24

Mishima Yukio, 45–64; aesthetic, foundation of, 53; appearance of, changes to, 56; classicism of, 56–58; death and love, beliefs about, 52; early death, fascination with, 49–51; emperor-worship of, 53–54; fame of, 45; on human life, 49; on intellectuals, faces of, 56; Japanese language, interest in, 70; Kawabata, name for, 30; military service, physical examination for, 51; name of, Keene's method of writing, 48; Nobel Prize, possibility of winning, 24–26; old age, response to approaching, 49–50; orthography, traditional, use of, 55; suicide of, 42, 45–46, 64; tradition, love of, 54–55; West, borrowing from, 55–56

WORKS: *After the Banquet* (*Utage no ato*), 57; *The Blue Period* (*Ao no jidai*), 57; for Bunraku puppet theater, 55; *Confessions of a Mask* (*Kamen no kokuhaku*), 48, 51; *The Decay of the Angel* (*Tennin Gosui*), 64; *The Fall of the House of Suzaku* (*Suzaku-ke no metsubō*), 55; farewell letters, 47–48; final, 45–46; heroes of, 52; *Introduction to* Hagakure (*Hagakure nyūmon*), 53; *Kinkakuji* (*The Temple of the Golden Pavilion*), 24–25, 52, 58–63; *Madame de*

Sade (Sado kōshaku fujin), 57; nō plays, 55; *Patriotism (Yūkoku)*, 52–53; *Runaway Horses (Homba)*, 52, 54, 63; *The Sailor Who Fell from Grace with the Sea (Gogo no eikō)*, 52; *The Sea of Fertility*, 48, 63–64; *The Sound of Waves (Shiosai)*, 56; *Spring Snow (Haru no yuki)*, 63; *tanka*, 46–47; *The Temple of Dawn (Akatsuki no tera)*, 63–64; "The Voices of the Heroic Dead" (Eirei no koe), 54

Mizoguchi (fictional character), 58–60
Mother of Captain Shigemoto, The (*Shōshō Shigemoto no haha*, Tanizaki), 19–20

Nagai Michio, vii–viii
"Nansen Kills a Cat" (*kōan*), 62–63
Naomi (Chijin no ai, Tanizaki), 10, 13
Naomiism, 13
nationalism, 91–92
"new Japanese," 92
New Sensationalists, 32–33
Nezu Matsuko, 15–16
nō plays, modern, 55
Nobel Prize for Literature, 23, 24–26

Ōe Kenzaburō, 26, 65
Ohisa (fictional character), 14
Old Capital, The (Koto, Kawabata), 26
One Arm (Kataude, Kawabata), 41, 42
Ono Yōko, 65
Ōoka Shōhei, 26
Oyū-san (fictional character), 16

Pass, The (Tōge, Shiba), 99
past, the, 7, 15, 17, 19

Patriotism (Yūkoku, Mishima), 52–53
poems, 46–47, 74–75
"Portrait of Shunkin, A" (Shunkin shō, Tanizaki), 16–17
puppet theater, 55

Racine, Jean, 57
Radiguet, Raymond, 49
"Red Cocoon, The" (Akai mayu, Abe), 77
"Reed Cutter, The" (Ashikari, Tanizaki), 16
Ruined Map, The (Moetsukita chizu, Abe), 75
Runaway Horses (Homba, Mishima), 52, 54, 63

sadomasochism, 8
Sailor Who Fell from Grace with the Sea, The (Gogo no eikō, Mishima), 52
Sasuke (fictional character), 17
Sea of Fertility, The (Mishima), 48, 63–64
Sebastian (saint), 51–52
Seidensticker, Edward, 2–3, 24
Seikichi (fictional character, tattooer), 7
Seiko (Tanizaki's sister-in-law), 8, 11
Self-Defense Force, 51
seppuku (ritual suicide), 45, 52, 53
Shiba Ryōtarō, 85–100; on *Asahi shimbun*, 93; Basques, interest in, 91–92; as hero, 96; internationalism of, 94; and Keene, 85–90, 99; languages, study of, 98; nationalism, dislike of, 91–92; personal qualities of, 99–100; on Tokugawa period, 90; Tsunoda,

Shiba Ryōtarō (*Continued*)
comparison with, 87–88; World
War II, effect on, 87; works of, in
bookshops, 96; writing style of, 97,
98–99
WORKS: *Drunk as a Lord* (*Yotte sōrō*),
97; historical fiction, 95, 97–98; *The
Pass* (*Tōge*), 99; reception of, 95–97,
98–99; *The Sound of Peoples' Footsteps* (*Hitobito no ashioto*), 99;
Storm Winds in Tartary (*Dattan
shippū roku*), 98; translations of, 97,
98–99
Shield Society (Mishima's private army),
46
Shimamura (fictional character), 38
Shimanaka Hōji, viii
shishi-odoshi (deer-frightener), 3
Shitennō-ji (temple), 88
short-short stories (*tanagokoro no shōsetsu*), 34
Shunkin (fictional character), 16–17
Snow Country (*Yukiguni*, Kawabata),
24, 34, 38–39
Some Prefer Nettles (*Tade kuu mushi*,
Tanizaki), 14
Sound of Peoples' Footsteps, The (*Hitobito no ashioto*, Shiba), 99
Sound of the Mountain, The (*Yama no
oto*, Kawabata), 24, 41
Sound of Waves, The (*Shiosai*, Mishima), 56
spirituality, Eastern, 13. *See also* Buddhism
Spring Snow (*Haru no yuki*, Mishima),
63
Storm Winds in Tartary (*Dattan shippū
roku*, Shiba), 98

Surrealism, 42
Swedish Academy, 25–26

Takeyama, Lieutenant (fictional character), 52–53
Tale of Flowering Fortunes, A (*Eiga
monogatari*, historical fiction), 94
Tale of Genji, The (Murasaki Shikibu),
17–18, 20, 40–41
Tale of the Heike (historical fiction),
94–95
tanagokoro no shōsetsu (short-short stories), 34
Tanizaki Jun'ichirō, 1–21; on art and
music, 8–10; on autobiographical
fiction, 4; early years of, 5; education
of, 5–6; films, interest in, 11; first
love of, 6; foot fetishism of, 7, 11; as
gourmet, 4; and Great Earthquake,
11; humiliation of, as servant, 6; on
joy, 6; Kansai region, move to, 12–
13; and Keene, 2, 3; lifestyle of, 11;
marriages of, 8, 15; men, lack of interest in, 3; military, hatred of, 18;
and Nezu Matsuko, 15–16; past, interest in, 7, 13–15; prizes won by, 19;
reverence for, 4; Tokyo, view of, 11–
12; at Tokyo Imperial University, 6;
West, attraction to, 8–10; on Western literature, influence of, 13–14
WORKS: *Amateur Club* (*Amachua kurabu*), 11; *Arrowroot* (*Yoshino kuzu*),
14–15; *A Blind Man's Tale* (*Mōmoku
monogatari*), 15; "The Boy Prodigy"
(*Shindō*), 6; "Children" (*Shōnen*),
8; *Diary of a Mad Old Man* (*Fūten
rōjin nikki*), 7, 20–21; "The German
Spy" (*Dokutan*), 8–10; "In Praise of